TH

Cover: Devonport and District tramcar (Brush No. 21) on "turnround" at St Budeaux Square. Transport staff were invariably proud to be photographed with their charges.

Plymouth Corporation ex-Devonport car, No.74, standing in Milehouse yard.

The TRAMS
of PLYMOUTH
a 73 Years Story

Martin Langley
and
Edwina Small

EX LIBRIS PRESS

Published in 1990 by
Ex Libris Press
1 The Shambles
Bradford on Avon
Wiltshire

Typeset by Manuscript, Trowbridge, Wiltshire
Printed by BPCC Wheatons, Ltd., Exeter

ISBN 0 948578 25 4

By the same authors and published by Ex Libris Press:

Wells: an Historical Guide (1990)

About the authors:
Martin Langley is an ex-Plymouthian, who went to school daily by
tramcar, and eventually travelled in the last car to run. A one-time
mariner, he usually writes nautical books, but noting there was no book
devoted to Plymouth's trams, he determined, having had a long
association with them, to supply what was lacking.
Edwina Small is the Estimator's clerk in a well-known West Country
building firm. Although having never experienced travel on a Plymouth
tram, she is very familiar with Plymouth, and entered with enthusiasm
into the research for this book.

CONTENTS

INTRODUCTION

Nostalgia is probably the reason for this book; and the realisation that the Trams of Plymouth, although reviewed in several books on street transport, have never had a book to themselves. Well, they have now.

Plymouth was first in Britain with a tramway system, following the Liberal Government's Tramways Act of 1870; and — because of World War II — was one of the last cities to have trams running. Their future, as a unified system, seemed assured at the union of the Three Towns in 1914, and reached its apogee as Plymouth attained city status in 1928. In 1941 the trams shared Plymouth's darkest hours, and bore the scars.

But throughout Britain, corporations and companies alike had no vision of a tramways future nor ever seriously experimented with their development — and Plymouth was no exception. Abroad, conversely, other countries did realise the potential of tramway systems and have benefitted accordingly.

It is now nearly forty-five years since Plymouth streets echoed to the clatter of the trams' progress, the deep hum of their motors, and the low swish of their trolley arms. It is a music we shall not hear again. But with it passed a form of street transport more commodious, less prone to failure, and offering cheaper travel than its successors. Not only so, but Plymouth trams at their best — especially those serviced at Prince Rock — actually provided a much quieter and smoother ride than the buses we know today.

Martin Langley
Edwina Small

PREAMBLE

Modern Plymouth was originally formed when the old boroughs of Plymouth, Stonehouse and Devonport were united in 1914. The history of Plymouth's tramways is somewhat complex in that these three towns formed the setting; three tramway systems were involved, one of which changed hands twice; and three forms of motive power were variously employed. Even the titles of the original companies contribute to the confusion, as each gives an exaggerated idea of its actual working area, while the constant repetition of their respective initials (PS&D, PD&D, PTC, D&D) becomes an exercise in tongue-twisting or glazing of the eyes.

This book is an attempt to tell the story simply, with the aid of sketch maps, in chronological sequence of forms of motive power and the emergence of the three systems. For convenience, and ease of under-standing, the Plymouth, Stonehouse and Devonport Tramways Company Ltd. will be referred to throughout as the Stonehouse company; the Plymouth, Devonport and District Tramways Company Ltd. and its successors as the Plymouth company; and the Devonport & District Tramways Company Ltd. as the Devonport company.

The reader is invited to study the following tables before reading the text and to refer to them as may be helpful thereafter.

REFERENCE TABLES

Sequence of Motor Power:

1 **Stonehouse company** (Green cars)
Horse traction, 1872 - 1901: 29 years
2 **Plymouth company** (Brown cars)
Steam traction, 1882 - 1885 (?): 3 (?) years
3 **Plymouth company & Corporation** (Red cars)
Horse traction, 1885 - 1899: 14 years
4 **Plymouth Corporation** (Red cars)
Electric & Horse traction, 1899 - 1907: 8 years
5 **Devonport company** (Brown cars)
Electric traction, 1901 - 1914: 13 years
6 **Stonehouse company** (Green cars)
Electric traction, 1901 - 1922: 21 years
7 **Plymouth Corporation** (Red cars)
Electric traction, 1907 - 1945: 38 years

The Three Systems:
The Stonehouse company (PS&D) were first in the field, — with horses, and they were the last to electrify.
The Plymouth company (PD&D; PTC) started ten years later, with steam trams, which ran for three or more years, although within three years they began changing to horse traction. The system (under PTC) was first to electrify.
The Devonport company (D&D) were last on the scene, but electric from the start.

Electric Tram Systems:
Three electric systems were operating 1901 - 14: 13 years
Two electric systems were operating 1914 - 22: 8 years
A single electric system operated 1922 - 45: 23 years

Electrification Dates:
Plymouth Corporation: 22 September, 1899
Devonport company: 26 June, 1901
Stonehouse company: 18 November, 1901

HORSE TRAMS
STONEHOUSE COMPANY: 1872 - 1901

Plymouth was one of the first places in Britain to operate a horse tramway. This was when the grandiosely named Plymouth, Stonehouse & Devonport Tramways Company — the first to be formed after the Parliamentary Tramway Act of 1870 — opened its route in the Three Towns on the 18 March 1872. Klapper (*The Golden Age of Tramways* by G.Klapper: David & Charles, 1974) refers to the line as 'the grandfather of all legitimate tramway companies.' It was the only system in Plymouth to be built to the railway gauge of 4'8½" and the distance originally run was 1 mile 74 chains. The line ran from Derry's Clock Plymouth to Cumberland Gardens Devonport via Union Street and Stonehouse Bridge, and the Company's activities were limited to this one route which was single track with eight passing places. Within twelve months this company became a subsidiary of the Provincial Tramways Company, which was also operating in Cardiff and Portsmouth.

In 1874 the route was extended at the Devonport end to the junction of Fore Street and Marlborough Street, with a one-way system — inwards via Chapel Street, outwards via St. Aubyn Street — which involved a crossover in Cumberland Street and increased the route distance to 2½ miles. Lower fares were charged on the open top deck, and up to six 'straphanger' passengers were allowed to stand inside — except on Devonport Hill, the gradient from Stonehouse Bridge to Mount Wise cricket ground. Here trace horses were attached to assist cars in the westbound direction, and standing passengers were banned in either direction. Each tram passing the 'ha'penny gate', as the bridge was called locally, was recorded by the tollkeeper for later reimbursement by the company.

Stonehouse (PSD) company's 4'8½" gauge car at the Octagon, westbound, in the 1880's. Visibly a more substantial vehicle than the Plymouth (PDD) company's 3'6" gauge cars. The picture shows how the horses were coupled to the tram by a central shaft: in some towns they were coupled only by harness, thereby losing any braking control. The tram driver had to be vigilant on the handbrake to avoid over-running them in emergencies. It can be seen that on the 4'8½" gauge the horses walked inside the rails; on the narrow gauge they had to avoid treading on the rail. (Photo — the late W.J. Vanstone)

Stonehouse car starting to climb Devonport Hill. Of the five horses, two have come from Derry's Clock, two were attached below Stonehouse Bridge, and an extra trace has just come on at Richmond Walk. The two 'boys' minding the extra horses are hitching a lift on the driver's platform. The other carriage is not so adequately horsed, and one horse is having drastic encouragement! It was here, years later, that driver Tom Piper struggled with his runaway eastbound electric train. (Photo — the late F.S.Blight)

The track was laid with 84 lb rail. The maximum gradient was the 1 in 11 on Devonport Hill, and the sharpest curve, Fore Street/Chapel Street, of thirty-four feet radius. The original eight tramcars were open-topped with 'knifeboard' seating, and records show that in the year ending June 1880 the Stonehouse Company had carried over one million passengers, had made a satisfactory net profit of over £1800, and its eight cars and seventy-eight horses had travelled 134,724 route miles. With increasing traffic the original cars were replaced by twelve trams of greater capacity, some of which had traverse seating on top. Weight being a critical factor, the cars had only a railing around the end platforms, *i.e.* no shield or dashboard.

The horses which supplied the motive power were a smaller breed than the massive Shire horses which modern displays have taught us to associate with heavy haulage. A day's work was about ten to twelve miles, which meant they could do the return journey on the Stonehouse company's route twice before being rested. The work was arduous because although the wheel tyres ran on smooth rails, grit frequently clogged the rail recess and created considerable friction. The company used a primitive water cart to alleviate this condition. It discharged water from a tank through rear pipes by gravity. The working life of tram horses was five years and they were then invariably put down. It was fortunate for the employers that horses were not costly to obtain, since a large number had to be retained, to allow for animals temporarily indisposed or lame, and for the regular use of 'trace' or 'chain' horses to provide extra power on inclines. Approaching Fore Street an extra horse was attached to assist cars up the steep section of Chapel Street. Two horses were employed on the level. Two others were attached in Edgcumbe Place, and one or two more at Richmond Walk, for assistance up Devonport Hill. At the top of the hill a 'trace' boy led them back to their station.

The depot, comprising the tram sheds and stables for the company's eventual 116 horses, was off Manor Lane, north of Union Street. The company's livery was a lightish green with white lining, and the service was popularly called the 'green trams'. Gentry recalls that the company suffered one major accident during the twenty-nine years of horse traction, on Devonport Hill, but no details have come to light. Doidge's *West Country Annual* for 1883 advertised the service as follows:

PLYMOUTH, STONEHOUSE, DEVONPORT, Etc. The first **TRAMWAY CAR** leaves **PLYMOUTH** on Week Days at 8.30 am; **DEVONPORT** at 8.45 am and every ten minutes up to 10 am. From 10 am to 9 pm every five minutes, and from 9 pm to 10.30 pm every ten minutes.

Fares: Between Plymouth & Edgcumbe St. siding, Stonehouse, and vice-versa. Inside 1½d Outside 1d.
any part of Stonehouse and Devonport, and vice-versa, Inside 2d Outside 1½d.
any part of Plymouth and Devonport, and vice-versa, Inside 3d Outside 2½d.

Children over 3 years of age must pay the full fare.

SUNDAYS. The tram cars run on Sundays from 1.15 pm to 10.15 pm.

In 1895 an acrimonious dispute developed between the tramway directors and the General Toll Company over the Stonehouse Bridge tolls. The practice had been for the tram-boy, whose three trace horses had assisted the tram horses on the up gradient, to bring them back via the tollgate at a lower rate, as led horses. The General Toll Company apparently objected to this seemingly fair arrangement, but the matter was eventually settled by an adjustment in the sum to be paid to the Toll Company by the Tramway. Twenty-nine years were to pass before the bridge was freed of toll, and though by then the Stonehouse company was no more, it would have been fitting if one of its erstwhile trams had been deputed to grace the ceremony. In the event, the Tramways Committee could not resist using one of their newly-acquired vestibuled 'square-faces' to break the ceremonial tape.

STEAM TRAMS
PLYMOUTH COMPANY: 1882 - 1889

In 1882, ten years after the Stonehouse company's route opened, another company was formed, with powers to operate steam trams; and destined, despite an unpromising start, to become the only surviving concern, as Plymouth Corporation Tramways. This was the Plymouth, Devonport and District Tramways Company Ltd., which, authorised by an Act of the same year, attempted to establish a system of tramways covering Devonport, Stoke, Plymouth, Mutley, Compton and Plympton. Its authorised capital was £125,000 and the mileage of authorised lines was ten and a half, nearly all single track. Seven lines were sanctioned, of which three served Devonport (*see* sketch map enclosed). The sole routes they originally operated were: from West Hoe to Hyde Park Corner, — by a circuitous route, to avoid the long climb up Tavistock Road from Old Town Street to North Hill —and a branch line to the Barbican. The gauge was 3'6" and it was this gauge which was to prevail in Plymouth. The width of vehicles was restricted to 5'6"and speed on the roads not to exceed 8 m.p.h.

The passenger cars were not powered. Eight four-wheeled trailer trams — apparently some double, some single deck — were acquired and five separate haulage units. These latter were Wilkinson vertical-boilered 0-4-0 steam locomotives of a well-tried design — two hundred similar engines were in use about the country. Designed by a William Wilkinson of Wigan, they were entirely boxed in from a few inches above rail level to the waist, and had a tall funnel projecting from their roof which was nine feet above rail level. The open driving platforms at either end duplicated the controls, and both hand and steam brakes were fitted. The cylinders appear to have been mounted vertically, the final drive on to 2'6" diameter wheels being taken by a reduction gearing of two or two and a half to one.

The company's livery was brown and white, the tram-engines being brown only and the trailer trams having white side-panels and brown dashes. The depot was in West Hoe Road, Millbay and thirty years after the demise of steam trams a short piece of track was still in situ, leading to a cobbled courtyard where the pattern of the setts clearly showed the site of a small turntable.

The Plymouth, Devonport and District Tramways Act of 1882 had authorised construction of the following lines:

1. *One and a half miles:* Russell Street to Compton Lane, via Richmond Street, Coburg Street, North Road, Houndiscombe Road, Mutley Plain.
2. *Four and a half miles:* Russell Street to the Plymouth Inn, Ridgeway, Plympton, via Cornwall Street, East Street, Treville Street, Exeter Street.
3. *One mile:* Russell Street to West Hoe, via Westwell Street, Princess Square, and Millbay Station.
4. *Half-mile:* Princess Square to Brunswick Inn, Barbican, via Notte Street and Southside Street.
5. *One and a half miles:* Russell Street to Fore Street (Devonport) via Morley Street, Cambridge Street, Oxford Street, Sidney Street, Pennycomequick, Deadlake Lane (now Stuart Road) and Paradise Place.
6. *Three-quarters mile:* Wingfield Villas Bridge to Albert Road (Railway Inn) via Osborne Villas & Upper Portland Road (Devonport).
7. *Three-quarters mile:* junction with No. 5 to the top of Ford Hill via Trafalgar Road and Tavistock Road (Devonport).

All this track was to be single line, with passing loops, and the provision for steam traction - or other mechanical power — was subject to the consent of the Board of Trade. The use of certain streets was also conditional upon consent of the local authorities concerned. A further Act of 1884 renewed the powers.

The Plymouth company had therefore an ambitious programme of routes with the hub of the system in the erstwhile Russell Street and they proceeded rapidly with laying down the tracks for most of Routes 1, 3 & 4. (The intended terminus of Route 4 at Brunswick Inn on the Barbican itself was cut back, on Corporation objection, to the Yarmouth Inn in Southside Street.) But they ran into early trouble with their first service, West Hoe to Hyde Park Corner. This route had been laid as follows: Millbay Road - George Street - Lockyer Street - Princess Square - Westwell Street - Bedford Street - Richmond Street - Coburg Street - North Road - Houndiscombe Road - Mutley Plain. The Board of Trade inspector would not pass the use of the Track through Richmond Street which was a narrow thoroughfare on a fairly steep gradient. Some trial runs were made to Mutley but thereafter the system was effectively cut into two parts, neither of them financially viable without through running.

Nor was this the company's only worry. There were widespread complaints, aired in the local press and voiced at meetings of the Corporation, of unreliable timekeeping, of thick black smoke and unpleasant fumes from the tram engines, and excessive noise in operation. According to Sambourne, these difficulties obliged the owners to sell out after only twelve months operation; but no confirmation of this claim has come to light and no new company name is recorded. Certainly not all Plymothians were so dissatisfied. A former passenger on the steam trams, H. Shapcote, wrote years later:

> The cars went from Russell Street to the end of Notte Street and to West Hoe. I was in two trips. The cars were white at the side and brown at the ends and under parts. The engines were 0-4-0 painted brown with the wheels covered up. The cars had one deck. They ran very smoothly ....

The ban on Richmond Street and a complaining public were not, however, the only obstacles met by the company. The Preamble of the Plymouth & Devonport (Extension) Transport Act, 1886, identifies the straw which broke the camel's back. It reveals that the company had built lines One, Three and parts of Four at a cost of £50,000, but that Plymouth Corporation had objected to construction of parts of lines Two and Four; also that Devonport Corporation had obtained an injunction, dated 6 December, 1884, restraining the Company from operating any of their tramways until lines Five, Six and Seven — which would have served Devonport — had been constructed. Unable to raise the capital for these works, the company had perforce gone into liquidation, in 1885. The 1886 Act therefore authorised a new company, The Plymouth Tramways Company Ltd., to take over the lines already constructed and to build the Devonport lines, though with some modification of route.

It appears that in fact none of this new construction was put in hand, and the only immediate results of the 1886 Act seem to have been: the introduction of horse trams on some sections of the old lines; the abandonment of the section through Russell Street and Richmond Street, to placate the Board of Trade; and the closure of the branch to the Barbican; — retrenchment rather than advance.

It is not clear precisely when steam trams ceased to operate in Plymouth. B.Y.Williams considers it 'safe to assume that steam traction ceased on issue of the 1884 injunction.' Gentry (*The Tramways of the West of England*: Light Railway Transport League, 1952 & 60) says steam trams were withdrawn in 1885. The fact is that we do not know, and it is possible that the new company replaced them gradually with horse traction. They were, after all, new vehicles of a type apparently well proven elsewhere, and the company were unprovided with stabling. It is likely, however, that there was no steam traction after 1884. The five Wilkinson tram engines were eventually sold to Swanscombe Colliery in Kent, where they continued to work, stripped of bodywork, roof and tall funnel, until 1922.

3

HORSE TRAMS
PLYMOUTH COMPANY: 1885 - 1899
(Corporation from 1892)

The new Plymouth company acquired twelve new horse trams from an unknown source, and these were in service for fifteen years. Sambourne declares that the livery of the Plymouth Tramways Company's fleet 'is unknown', but Gentry says 'the cars were painted red and cream with the name in full on the lower rocker panel and coat of arms on the upper.' Time-keeping continued to be bad, because the narrow streets of the time were congested with other horse traffic. The complaints of the public eventually goaded the Corporation to take action. They paid £12,500 to take the company over, and formed the Plymouth Corporation Tramways Department to run the system. The year was 1892, and C. R. Everson was appointed General Manager.

There is some doubt whether the Corporation purchased any new rolling stock immediately, but in their first year of operation they had available both two-horse open-toppers, and one-horse single-deck 'toastrack' cars, probably all inherited from their predecessors.

By the 11 March 1893 the Millbay-Mutley route had been extended southward to West Hoe Basin (terminus in Pier Street), and on 3 April that year northward to Compton (Compton Lane End) from Hyde Park Corner. Meanwhile, in addition to the old steam tram depot at Millbay, car sheds and stables were established in Lower Compton Lane and at Belgrave Mews, Mutley.

The latter was rented, and used for the stabling of trace horses required for Townsend Hill. The Compton, Mutley and Millbay stables had to accommodate 250 horses.

The date of the official commencement of Corporation running is uncertain, but on 7 October 1945 (a week after the last Plymouth tram had run) the *Western Independent* printed the following:

THE FIRST DRIVER

It now appears that the real veteran at the Last Tram ceremony was Mr George Slater, of 27 Headland Park, who is 84, and drove the first Plymouth Corporation tram (horsedrawn) way back in 1893.

Mr Slater whipped up his gee-gees at Compton Lane End, near the then tram stables, and drove them on a twenty minutes historic ride to Plymouth Market.

The tram had 12 passengers inside and twelve on top. The fare was 1d, so that each journey was worth a maximum of 2s to the infant transport undertaking.

In those early days there were 4 trams and four drivers, of whom Mr Slater is the sole survivor. He earned 'the magnificent sum' of a guinea a week.

Five new cars, nos. 13 - 17 were delivered from Milnes of Birkenhead in 1894; two were single-deck and three were open-toppers. The Corporation livery was now established as Vermilion red, with white window-frames, and gold-lined. Two further open-toppers, nos. 18 and 19, were obtained from Milnes in 1895. The section G.P.O. Westwell Street to the top of Richmond Street, virtually disused since the Board of Trade inspector's disapproval in 1883, had been disconnected, and a new line laid from the top of Richmond Street through Pound Street and Old Town Street to Market Avenue, with a terminus by the Pannier Market.

In 1895 a further route to Mutley Plain was opened, via Tavistock Place — passing St. Luke's Church — and Tavistock Road, over North Hill, the two routes dividing at the Duke Street/Clarence Street crossing, which later became known as Spear's Corner. The trace horses for Tavistock and North Hill were stabled at Belgrave Mews. The Tavistock Place track was later diverted to Tavistock Road.

There was a serious accident on 12 June 1896, when the two year old son of Mr and Mrs Hatherleigh (of the Nottingham Inn, Mutley Plain) stumbled and fell under a tram at Braidwood Terrace, North Hill, and was instantly killed.

On 28 August 1896, street widening made it possible to rejoin the two ends of the severed line, tracks being laid from Market Avenue through Old Town Street and Basket Street to the G.P.O., Westwell Street. On the 10 December the same year the tracks of a new route (not one of those specified by the 1882 Act, but by an Order of 1893) were laid to Prince Rock. They diverged from the Compton route at the point which in 1904 became Drake Circus, and continued via Ebrington Street, Friary Bridge, Tothill Road and Embankment Road.

Meanwhile the decision had been taken to convert the system to electric traction, so pending the change-over no further extensions were contemplated. Trams on the Compton route soon found themselves in competition with Baskerville's Buses, which had a service from Derry's Clock to Mannamead. There were two incidents, *c.* 1898, one involving horse tram No. 16, and the other horse tram No. 17, when buses and trams came into sidelong collision. Whether by accident or intent was never established; but though no one was hurt, some damage was inevitably sustained, and the Corporation threatened Baskerville with legal action if there was a recurrence. It appears there was not, so one may draw one's own conclusions.

4

ELECTRIC and HORSE TRAMS
PLYMOUTH COMPANY   1899 - 1901

The Plymouth Corporation Tramways Department received authorisation in 1898 to convert to electric traction, but it was a year later before the first route was ready to operate. The hub of the system became the west end of George Street, outside the Theatre Royal, beyond Derry's Clock. It became known simply as 'Theatre' on route indicators and on tickets.

The new Prince Rock route was chosen for the initial electrification, later to be familiar to several generations of Plymothians as Route 5. A four-road car shed for twenty-eight trams was built in Elliot Road, Prince Rock, and a generating station nearby on the shore of Cattewater harbour, as the Tramway was to supply its own power. This powerhouse was in fact the beginning of the Plymouth Corporation Electricity Department, and led to the town's first electric street lighting. Prince Rock was the system's largest depot until 1922.

The service opened on 22 September 1899 with a procession of the first cars delivered, nos. 1 - 6 driven in file and beflagged, from Prince Rock to Market Avenue. (A few lengths of rail could still be seen in Market Avenue about eighteen years later.) Car no. 1 was driven by motorman W.A.Smith, who little guessed that he was destined also to be on the last electric tram to run, forty-six years later. These six forty-two seater cars, built by Milnes of Birkenhead, were unbalconied, short-canopy open-toppers with direct, half-turn stairs and four side-windows, mounted on short-wheelbase Peckham cantilever trucks, — and their ancestry from horse trams was evident. All were to remain in service for twenty-five years. In the first year of electrification one million passengers were carried. Electrification of the Market Avenue to Theatre section was probably completed within a year. At Theatre, guardrails were in later years erected to form waiting passengers into

About 1895: the horse car is on the Westwell street to West Hoe service. Note single line track and hansom cab on the cab rank, passing Derry's Clock, one of the few landmarks to survive the war damage and subsequent rebuilding of the city centre. (Photo — the late F.S.Blight)

About 1924: picture showing the queuing arrangements of guard rails and route indicators built where the cab rank had been. The car No.96 on Route 7 has just arrived, but its indicator has already been turned to 'South Keyham'.

queues, with the route number displayed over each entry point. This was the tramways centre which older Plymothians will remember, and which served until 1941.

The following year, 1900, a further fourteen cars, numbered 7 to 20, were obtained from the Brush Company of Loughborough. They also were four-window cars on Peckham cantilever trucks, but they were balconied and fitted with reverse-direction stairs. All except nos. 22 and 26, which outlasted their sisters by ten years, served until 1924.

Of these first twenty cars — no concession was made to superstition over no. 13 — the first six were fitted for towing, and in peak traffic periods towed trailer trams (actually horse car conversions) as was common in London (which had 150 purpose-built trailers) during the Great War and early 'twenties. Trailer trams were discontinued in Plymouth after one became uncoupled in Old Town Street, left the track, and crashed into a shop window. Towing gear was removed from nos. 1 - 6 after an accident in which a young cyclist, trying to 'hitch' a ride, died from his injuries. It was replaced by Tidswell Patent safety-guards — wooden slatted frames which scooped anything from the track, and which became standard on all cars. Nos. 1 - 6 did not have the handwheel operated track brake, though photographs suggest they were fitted with electric magnetic brakes. On this account they were used only on the Prince Rock and, later, Beaumont Road routes, which were virtually level. Nos. 7 - 20 did however have the handwheel-worked mechanical track brakes.

The arrival of these fourteen cars made possible the operation of further routes, and the original town — Compton route opened with electric traction on 4 April 1901, with a terminus at the junction of the Tavistock and Egg Buckland roads that became known to several generations as Hender's Corner. The horse tram depot in Lower Compton Road was enlarged, to consist of a tram shed and overhaul works, with the Tramway Manager's residence, Kelvin House, adjacent. There was accommodation for sixteen cars — four roads under cover, five in the yard — and a traverser. The Mutley trace-horses' stables at Belgrave Mews were now sold, and a sub-station erected in Armada Street to boost the current for cars ascending Tavistock Road.

Despite the injunction obtained by Devonport Corporation in 1884 to prevent a Plymouth company from building a system without lines to Devonport, neither the 1886 Plymouth Tramways Company nor the 1892 Corporation Tramways Department had as yet shown any inclination to oblige their Devonport neighbours.

Plymouth Corporation 3'6" gauge horse tram at the turnstile of the Promenade Pier, on the Theatre — West Hoe route. The painted route description baord shows that the car normally worked between Market Place and Compton Lane End. (Photo — the late F.S.Blight)

Car No.20 (Plymouth Corporation, series 7-20) introduced 1901. In the early 'twenties this class had the wheelbase extended by cutting the truck frame in the middle and welding in a new 6" section. No.20 was one of the last survivors of the class and was latterly used as a Football Special on Argyle's 'home' Saturdays.

One of the single-deck, one-horse cars used until 1907 on the West Hoe route.

About 1910: single deck car No. 41 on the Pennycomequick to Hoe and Piers service. Cab rank and shelter still extant.

The track on the Plymouth system was of 92 lb rail, except in a few places — *e.g.* Radford Road — where lighter rail (for demi-cars?) was never replaced. The sharpest curve was of thirty-five feet radius in Princess Square, rounding the Repertory Theatre, and the maximum gradient was 1 in 9 on Saltash Road, passing North Road station.

Horse trams continued to operate on the Beaumont Road, Peverell, Pennycomequick and West Hoe routes. West Hoe was served mainly by single-deck 'toastrack' cars with canvas side curtains, and drawn by a single horse. They started from a spur in Westwell Street opposite the Liberal Club, where for years could be seen the rusting remains of the track over which steam trams had formerly puffed their way through Bedford Street into Russell Street. These single-deckers used the electrified lines around the Mechanic's Institute (later the Repertory Theatre) into Princess Square — often causing considerable delays — until they reached Theatre, where the lines to Millbay and West Hoe remained unelectrified till 1907. The horse trams had no headlamp. For night operation, two oil lanterns in the saloon, one behind each bulkhead, shone a fitful light through a bulls eye lens, and a red glass swivelled over this for a rear light. This system persisted in the earlier electric trams, until the arrival of the 31 - 36 class, with large headlamps on the dashes, in 1905. The 131 series were the first with good rear red lamps which could easily be seen.

5

ELECTRIC TRAMS
DEVONPORT COMPANY, 1901 - 1914

By the turn of the century Devonport Corporation and the people of Devonport, long disenchanted with being the Cinderella of the Three Towns in the matter of modern transport, at last had cause to rejoice. The Devonport & District Tramways Company was registered in 1898 and secured powers to build five miles of track within the borough.

This company had been spawned by the British Electric Traction Company (BET), formed in 1896 by Emile Garcke, German-born, naturalised English tramways entrepreneur. Its function was to promote provincial tramway companies which though individually financed, were controlled by BET who appointed the managing board, supplied the engineering back-up, and ordered their rolling-stock and equipment from the Brush Company of which Garcke was managing director. Since the authorised lines did not reach to the outskirts of Devonport, the Corporation in 1900 obtained powers for a further four miles of line, reaching to Tor Lane (beyond Peverell) and Saltash Passage. The Devonport company employed only electric power from the outset, provided by the Devonport Corporation generating station beside Stonehouse Creek; and commenced running services on 26 June 1901. The gauge was 3'6" and the five initial routes, totalling four and three-quarters miles, were based on a headquarters (office, depot and workshops) at Milehouse. The routes were:

Morice Square to Camels Head *via* Keyham Road and Saltash Road;
Fore Street to Pennycomequick *via* Paradise Road and Stuart Road;
Paradise Road to Milehouse *via* Trafalgar Road and Tavistock Road;
South Keyham to Trafalgar Road *via* Albert Road;
Albert Road to Paradise Road *via* Exmouth Road and Tamar Terrace.

Twenty-five cars were ordered to run these services, all delivered in 1901. The initial twenty were American-built, three-window, open-top trams with short canopies and direct stairs; both bodies and trucks by the J.G.Brill Car Company, Philadelphia. (This was because at that time the Brush company could not cope with the boom in tramcars.) A unique feature was that the roof was hollow, and the sash-type windows of the saloon could be opened, to disappear within the roof, between roof and ceiling. This feature was used by Brill to meet extreme hot weather conditions in America, where these cars were known as 'convertibles'. In the early days of operation the Devonport company occasionally opened these windows in heat wave conditions: but this was never done in Plymouth days when the leather tags for lifting the windows were removed, so that until altered the windows remained as loose sashes which rattled! The driver's controls were by Thompson Houston, with a reversing key and a brass control handle with wooden grip; when the driver changed ends at a terminus he took both these fittings with him, which intrigued passengers who were not 'in the know'. An excess load switch was fitted which automatically cut out when current consumption exceeded a certain figure. The last five tram cars delivered had five windows a side, and were Brush cars, acquired second-hand from a B.E.T. company in Bimingham.* Whereas the American-built cars had mechanical slipper track brakes, operated by a separate horizontal control wheel on the driver's left, the Brush cars had the wheel on the same pillar as the hand brake. The livery of the Devonport company was a rich chocolate-brown and cream, with the magnet-and-wheel crest of BET in the centre of the upper side panel.

Clearly the Devonport company meant business, and the Corporation, whose lines when completed were unconnected and little more than extensions to the above routes, handed over their tracks to the Company in 1903, after some wrangling over terms, for operation under lease. The Corporation's two tracks were: North Keyham to Tor Lane, Peverell, and Camel's Head to Saltash Passage. The latter was physically isolated from the rest of the system because Weston Mill Creek intervened, and the wooden bridge spanning it was not capable of bearing tram traffic. Two tramcars (nos. 22 and 24) shedded at a small Camel's Head depot, worked a shuttle service to and from the Saltash ferry, and passengers transferring to or from the Morice Square trams had to cross the bridge on foot. An embankment however was under construction, and on its completion the tracks were joined and a through service began. With the augmentation of the two Corpora-

---

* see illustration of No.21, on cover.

tion lines, the Devonport company now ran services as follows:

> Fore Street and Tor Lane, Peverell
> Fore Street and Pennycomequick
> Pennycomequick and Saltash Passage
> Morice Square and Saltash Passage
> Morice Square and Tor Lane (*via* St. Levan Rd.)

All these tracks were laid with 97 lb rail. The maximum gradient was 1 in 10 at Tamar Terrace, and the sharpest curve was of fifty feet radius, from the top of Albert Road, south into Trafalgar Road.

The Devonport company's Rules and Regulations for motormen and conductors raise a smile when we read them today and would be unlikely to find favour with Union stewards:

Motormen and conductors ... should be attentive to duty, care fully observing every person as they proceed along the streets, and if they notice anyone standing looking at the cars, undecided whether or not to ride, make a motion with their hands to attract their attention, which would many times induce them to ride, and thereby increase the business of the company.

They must, when standing at a terminus, and when approaching intending passengers, announce in a clear and distinct tone of voice, the route and destination of their car.

Disparaging remarks by the employees about the management of the routes, or about the officers of the Company will not be allowed, and will be regarded as a breach of the rules.

They must not enter into unnecessary conversation with the passengers, nor make signs, motions or signals of any kind to men in charge of other cars.

Between 1904 and 1906 the company seemed to be having difficulty in pleasing their public. Moseley states (*The History of Transport in Plymouth* by Brian S. Moseley: Mosbic, 1964): 'Complaints were numerous around this period.' In January 1904 there was a complaint that car no. 21 had been unduly noisy passing Milehouse, and the same car was complained of again in March. Then followed protests about unclean workmen's cars, and failure to adhere to timetables. The latter complaints were met belatedly in 1906 by the posting of time schedules in all tram shelters — as a spur it seems, to tram crews. Before 1904 was out the Devonport Corporation were demanding a more frequent service between Fore Street and Milehouse. In January 1905 it became necessary to post 'Spitting Prohibited' notices in all cars following complaints and from March to July letters were coming about noisy trams; — cars 14, 17, 2 and 8 being respectively the specific offenders. In 1906 it was the turn of the company themselves to make a complaint; they requested the Police to stop children from running after cars and hitching a lift on the buffer below the dash. (In one such case a Morice Town School boy lost an arm when he fell under the tram's rear wheel.) At a Tramways Committee meeting in June a complaint was received that cars were descending Stoke Hill too fast. Months followed when the Corporation were demanding certain fares be decreased and the Company consistently refused on the grounds that they could not sustain the loss of revenue.

Although it appears that the Company gradually placated the public, by 1908 an intermittent war was being waged with both the Devonport and Plymouth Corporations. The Devonport Corporation tried to insist on timetable changes, improved service frequencies, and additional early morning workmen's cars; and the company resisted strongly, despite in 1909 being taken to the Divisional Court and being fined on certain counts. The atmosphere between the Company and Devonport Corporation became steadily worse up to the outbreak of war. Toward the Plymouth Corporation the Company adopted a more tactful and conciliatory approach. They desired to expand, especially from Tor Lane to Crownhill, and they wanted through running; but Plymouth Corporation were determined they should have neither, and maintained a hostile attitude.

On 6 May 1908 tramcar no. 25 was stopped by the Police at 5.10 pm for being grossly overloaded. The Chief Constable complained that eighty-two passengers were on board, 'being 36 in excess'. In 1909 the Company withdrew services over the two lines leased from the Corporation as unremunerative, but had to restart them following a fine and a Court order. To this rebuff the Company reacted commercially by opening Tea Gardens at Little Ash on the St. Budeaux - Saltash Passage route - a venture which proved very successful. Indeed the inauguration of all-in tickets for a round trip to the tea gardens by tram and return by boat, or vice-versa, greatly improved the revenue on the Saltash Passage service.

Two more batches of tramcars were delivered in 1911. The first four, nos. 26 to 29, were balconied, direct stairs Brush bodies on Brush 'A' trucks. The last four, nos. 30 - 33 were the only Devonport Company cars to have reversed stairs. All eight were purchased from Birmingham and other BET companies, and were probably second-hand vehicles.

Klapper (*The Golden Age of Tramways*: David & Charles, 1974.) describes the cars of the Devonport fleet as 'all of antique appearance'. This was so inasmuch as they were rather small at a time when trams elsewhere were tending to be built larger; and 1 - 25 remained unbalconied until modernised, post-war, by Plymouth Corporation. All the Devonport company's cars were distinguished by roller-blind indicators mounted high above the upper-deck guardrails — but no route numbers - and the headlamps of 1 - 25 were on the canopies. Coloured lights were displayed after dark, for route identification, from February 1914, as follows:

Fore Street to Tor Lane: Red light
Fore Street to Stuart Road: White
Stuart Road to Keyham: Red
Morice Square to St. Budeaux: Red
Morice Square to Tor Lane: White

Punch-drunk with complaints though the Company must have been by 1911, absurdity was reached in July when the Devonport Corporation forwarded a letter received from the London & South Western Railway. This demanded financial acknowledgemehnt for the 'light and air' gained over the railway's property by four windows in the Camel's Head tram depot! The Company were determined not to fall for this one. It was decided the shed was light enough without the windows, and they were promptly boarded up.

During its fourteen year independent career the Company suffered a number of dramatic accidents. The first would appear to have been during the first year of operation, and occurred where three of the other four accidents took place — the junction of Tamar Terrace with Paradise Road. *The Western Morning News*, referring later to this accident without dating, records that 'the car jumped the rails at the curve, and ran into the wall above the road leading to the (LSWR) station.' There were no casualties and the tram seems not to have been capsized.

Three accidents occurred on the system in 1902. In the January a tram descending Albert Road lost braking power, jumped the track at the foot of the hill and careering across William Street, hit a tree in Sparrow Park after demolishing a shelter. Some youngsters who had been loitering in the shelter ran clear in time, and there was no loss of life.

On 3 June that year car No. 8, running between Camel's Head and Stuart Road, passed east of the Devonport Technical Schools and in turning left onto the main road toppled over toward the LSWR station, striking a GWR horse wagon as it did so. The car was carrying about sixteen passengers, evenly distributed on top and inside. Miraculously, none suffered serious injury. The conductor, William Longman, was taken to the Royal Albert Hospital with a broken ankle, and the driver of the GWR wagon sustained a leg injury. Strangely, one of three glass side windows on the underside was not broken! A large traction engine which had been exhibited at the Bath & West Show, chanced to be in the station yard with steam up, and was used to right the tram. Damage to the car included the bodywork strained, trolley arm broken, and front platform with controls badly battered. There was two hours delay to traffic before another car arrived to tow the casualty to Milehouse. A flintstone, scored as though by a tram wheel, was found beside the track and was thought to have been wedged in the rail groove, causing the derailment. There was no malfunction of brakes, the car was not travelling fast, and was described by those on board as overturning 'comparatively slowly'.

Three months later, on 27 September car No. 7, which had already passed the spot three times that day, came to grief with more serious consequences. The driver, named Oarhart, had halted for passengers at the compulsory stop of Stopford Place, at the top of Tamar Terrace hill. On restarting, he found the brakes were not slowing the car, and shouted a warning to his passengers. Conductor Robert Binmore was collecting top deck fares as the car passed St. Michael's Terrace, but had regained the platform as they reached the Technical Schools. He saw a crash was inevitable and jumped off opposite the college side-entrance. Driver Oarhart stuck bravely to his controls till the car reached the bottom of the hill. He jumped clear as they hit the curve, and avoided certain death by doing so. No. 7 derailed and hit the station road wall with a tremendous crash, audible far away. Over twenty feet of wall were demolished. The top deck passengers were thrown into the road. Among them was Herbert Chope, a thirty-two year old Plymouth

A peaceful late 'twenties scene. 1919-built Brush car No.96 on Route 6, passing Devonport Technical College with Devonport LSWR station on the right. Behind the car, between the Glebefield tree and the first of the two tram-standards, is the scene of three derailments suffered by the former Devonport company. (Photo — B.Y.Williams)

dentist, who was killed outright by a seven hundredweight block of granite (the base of a lamp standard) falling on to his head when the tram's canopy displaced it. There were no other deaths, but all the passengers were injured in some measure. Doctors from the Stonehouse Military Hospital were quickly on the scene and organised stretcher parties. Two Naval personnel, an engineer cadet and a warrant shipwright from H.M. cruiser *Arrogant* were taken by army ambulance to the Royal Naval Hospital; they had been hurled into the station road amongst the stonework of the demolished wall and tram fittings. The motorman explained that, alarmed by the tram's acceleration, he had applied the brake so tightly that the wheels locked and the car skidded along the metals. He had released and then re-applied the brakes, but again the wheels had locked. He had applied the emergency brake, and reversed the motors. J.W.Endean, the Devonport Tramways manager, found that the hand, slipper and electrical brakes were in perfect condition, and all were on to the fullest extent, while the motors had been reversed several points. Flat spots on the wheel tyres were evidence that the car had skidded down the hill when the brakes were applied. The car was righted by a team of horses with block and tackle rigged to a tree in Glebe Road. The fore end canopy and offside top-deck guardrails were removed before the car was towed to Milehouse. The Tramway asked that the road be widened by acquiring the corner of Glebe Field, which would enable them to re-lay the curve on a greater radius.

Twelve years were to pass before the same curve took its toll again. In the early morning of 27 November 1914, three months after the outbreak of war, car No. 25, loaded with 'dockyardees' returning home from nightshift, was the prey of misfortune. Again it was a case of losing brake control on the Tamar Terrace gradient. The car overturned when it met the curve and came to rest against the long-suffering wall of the station road. One man (Isaac Searle aged fifty-one) was killed outright and thirty-three were injured, of whom two died later. Although at least two books refer to the brakes failing, informed opinion is that there was probably mismanagement of the brakes rather than failure. The car was fitted with hand-operated slipper brake, also electric rheostatic brake on the wheels as well as handbrake on the wheels. The probability is that the driver locked the wheels with the handbrake on too hard, so that the car skidded, and this would preclude any electrical braking. It was in other words, a repeat of the last accident here. The driver, Alfred Choek and conductor William Riley, both of Pennycomequick, suffered only

Devonport company's car No.25 overturned after running down Tamar Terrace, seen in background. Left, Devonport Technical College. Foreground, retaining wall of LSWR statiuon roadway, 27 November, 1914. (Photo — R.C.Sambourne)

One of the Devonport 26-29 cars after coming into PCT ownership as No. 67. The bodywork appears unchanged but the modern control handle suggests that the motors and electrical equipment have been renewed. Devonport 30-33 were similar, but with reversed stairs.

minor injuries, but Choek was found covered with debris and badly shocked. Car no. 25 had its trolley arm and standard broken, front canopy distorted by 45°, and most of the top seats displaced, while the side on which it fell was much battered. Traffic was inconvenienced for most of the day as it was 4 pm before the tram was righted. This was achieved by a chain purchase rigged to a tree in the Glebe field, a steam lorry supplying the power. The lorry then hauled the car in the Stuart Road direction until re-railed, when it was towed back via Tamar Terrace to Milehouse by a car sent for the purpose. Since the previous accident the corner had been cut back and the rails relaid to a more generous radius, with a camber on the inner rail. This was probably a major reason that No. 25 did not run straight into the station-approach wall, as had No. 7 in 1902, but overturned against it.

Accidents were not the only hiccups to beset the smooth running of the Devonport company. During the first decade of the century an exceptionally high tide one evening brought seaweed into Stonehouse Creek which blocked the intakes of cooling water for the generators at the Corporation's 200 volt DC electricity station. They had to be shut down for several hours. When the current failed, bringing all cars to a standstill, passengers for Plymouth — where the 230 volt AC supply was unaffected — had to continue their journeys on foot. But imagine! ... unlit tramcars stranded all over Devonport!

In December 1913 the Company began issuing books of fourteen tickets for one shilling, for the use of schoolchildren.

In October 1914 the Three Towns merged into one — Plymouth; and the Devonport Company was bought out by Plymouth Corporation. All its thirty-three cars were transferred, those involved in accidents having been repaired. At the time of takeover, the Company was in process of changing its livery from chocolate and cream to dark green and cream, and a number of cars were running in the new colours. In compliance with the Government's fuel saving campaign, the St. Budeaux — Saltash Passage line and the upper section of Albert Road were closed for the duration of the war and some intermediate steps were cut out. The lighting of the cars was reduced to meet the semi-blackout conditions, and the canopy headlamps were removed. Whilst there was no fear of air attack in 1915, there was always the thought of sea attack from enemy forces in the Channel and particularly the activities of U-boats: therefore the top half of the saloon windows were painted over in blue, and wherever the trams could be visible from the sea — such as St. Michael's Terrace, Devonport — all lights were switched off and the cars proceeded in the dark! Meanwhile wartime conditions dictated that integration with the Plymouth tramways could only be achieved gradually, and until after the war the Devonport system retained its individual character.

Trying to recreate the scene from seventy or so years on, it is difficult not to feel some sympathy for the Devonport company. They had begun by laying stronger track (at 97 lb section) than their neighbours; their 'Rules and Regulations' at least suggest that they cared about their public image; they had accepted the responsibility for running a service which the Corporation had shirked, but were always on the receiving end of advice, demands, and solicitors' letters. Their tea gardens and constant efforts to reach Crownhill Showed they did not lack enterprise: but their story nevertheless is one of almost constant strife, and they suffered the worst accidents of the three systems. One wonders how much of this trauma they may have brought upon themselves.

6

ELECTRIC TRAMS
STONEHOUSE COMPANY: 1901 - 1922

In 1901 the Stonehouse company relaid the whole line for electric traction, on the overhead system, to the 3'6" gauge used by the Plymouth and Devonport concerns, and sold the eastern and western extremities of their line to the respective corporations of Plymouth and Devonport in which they lay. However they continued to work the whole line, having negotiated a twenty-one years lease for the two sections sold to the boroughs. Electric power within the Plymouth boundary (Derry's Clock to Manor Street) was supplied by Plymouth Corporation. The remainder of the route derived its power from the Devonport Corporation powerhouse in Newport Street.

To work the system, fifteen cars were obtained from Dick Kerr & Company, with Brill 21E trucks. They were open-top double-deckers with end balconies, three side-windows and — with one exception — had reversed stairs. They were numbered 1-12 and 14-15, while No. 16, with direct stairs and of more modern design, was a late arrival in 1916. Superstition prevailed sufficiently to exclude the use of No.13! Nos. 1-15 were forty-eight seaters (twenty-six upstairs) while No.16 carried 52 (thirty upstairs); and all were destined to outlast the company, surviving after modification in 1922, into the mid-thirties. All the cars were fitted with single headlamps on their balcony ends, and a turnover destination board was carried above the dash.

The light-green and white livery of the horse trams was retained, with a belt-and-buckle device surrounding the car number on the waist panel, and the company's full name emblazoned on the rocker panel. Manor Lane depot was now closed, and the electric trams housed in a new depot in Market Street at the corner with Peel Street. This had six roads and a traverser, and could accommodate eighteen cars. The company's engineer and manager at this time was H.Moreton (father of Dr.

Harry Moreton, organist of St. Andrew's, Plymouth, for seventy-three years), and the administrative offices were at 13, Edgcumbe Street, Stonehouse.

Some route and track alterations were made. One-way working into Devonport was reversed so that cars arrived in Fore Street via St. Aubyn Street and left via Chapel Street, thus obviating the crossover in Cumberland Street. A terminal spur to the west in Fore Street, used by the horse trams since 1874, and extending to the Marlborough Street/ Tavistock Street cross, was not electrified at this time, and appears from old photographs to have been lifted. The track was double on the Plymouth and Devonport sections, but single-and-loop through Stonehouse in Union Street.

On 27 September 1902, the same day as the fatal tram accident at Tamar Terrace, and only six hours later, the Stonehouse company had their share of tragedy. Car No. 11 was travelling east along Cumberland Street, and passing the Garrison Church, when a little girl of five, named Katie Bennett, ran out into the road. A woman screamed hysterically, and the driver, Thomas Biddick, braked sharply. He could have done no more but the child, knocked down by the buffer plate, passed under the guard and was partly under the pilot board in front of the wheels when the car stopped. Helped by his sixty-year-old conductor, Frederick Brooks, Biddick, aged thirty-two, managed to ease the child out without having to jack up the tram. Staff-surgeon W.A.Whitelegg, a passenger in the car, attended to the little girl, who was stretchered to the Royal Albert Hospital. Sadly, she was found dead on arrival, having severe injuries to her head and one arm.

Although no existing books or records seem to record the fact, Plymouth Corporation must have laid in a connection with their own track at Courteney Street; for in 1905 they made unexpected use of their acquisition of the Stonehouse company's line between Manor Street and Derry's Clock, to run trams on their Beaumont Road service right through to Manor Lane, the Plymouth boundary. The lines connecting the systems passed either side of Derry's Clock and in laying them Plymouth Corporation were within their rights, but it was an insensitive move, to say the least. The Stonehouse company were not surprisingly incensed and withheld their payment of rates until threatened with legal action. In the event this extension of Route 4 proved uneconomical and was withdrawn.

In or about 1912 the Stonehouse company were fortunate to escape a major accident when a car descending Devonport Hill ran away when

Plymouth, Stonehouse and Devonport tram No.3, passing over Stonehouse Bridge.

its brakes failed. The driver was a Tom Piper, who had qualified as a motorman after leaving his former employment as a pony-cart deliverer for Joyce's, the Devonport butchers. The renegade tram clattered over Stonehouse Bridge, Piper sticking grimly to the controls and stamping out a furious warning on his pedal bell. The toll keeper could only gape, open-mouthed. At the reverse curves into Union Street the car swayed alarmingly but it kept the rails and as it slowed on the level Piper managed to get enough brake pressure to bring it to a halt.

The Stonehouse company's route was the only one in the Three Towns to cross municipal boundaries. After leaving Derry's Clock, Plymouth, passengers were made infallibly aware of crossing the border by Meadowcroft's Drapery on the corner of Phoenix Street, whose large sign proclaimed 'The First Shop in Stonehouse'; and sometimes by small boys on the Stonehouse side of the street pulling faces at Plymouth policemen glaring impotently from the edge of their jurisdiction. The Devonport boundary was the 'ha'penny gate', so was adequately marked by the stop for trace horses at Richmond Walk.

Retired tug captain Stan Daymond of Stonehouse recalls clearly those days of the three systems:

To reach the North yard from Prince Rock you caught the red tram to the Royal (Theatre), then the green tram to Fore Street; then walked to Morice Square and caught the brown tram to St. Levan Gate. Each ride for one penny. It was a penny anywhere.

When, at the union of the Three Towns in 1914 the Devonport company was absorbed, the Stonehouse company, by virtue of its twenty-one year lease, continued to operate until 1922, though petty local politics prevented any through working. Throughout the Great War the Stonehouse company's route assumed special significance and importance, serving H.M.Dockyard and the Royal Sailors Rest in Fore Street, Raglan Army Barracks in Cumberland Road, and being the nearest public transport to the Royal Naval Hospital in Clarence Place. The service continued unrestricted until the 11 November 1918 when the Armistice celebrations created such crowds in Union Street that passage through them became too hazardous and damage to the cars from revellers was likely. They were sent back to Market Street depot and their crews allowed to join the merrymaking.

B.Y.Williams recalls that, about 1920, a car ascending Devonport Hill (bound for Fore Street) came to a standstill for traffic reasons and began to slide backwards on a greasy rail. The conductor was unable to drop sand, as this was activated by a treadle-pin which was always removed from the rear platform by the driver who took it with him, when changing ends to the front. The car continued to slither back, running into the car behind and both cars then continued the slide together!

Immediately after purchase by Plymouth Corporation in 1922, connections were laid in at Fore Street with the former Devonport company's line to Peverell, and at Derry's Clock the infamous connection previously noted was now relaid and put to undisputed use. The Fore Street spur was reinstated, extended almost to Marlborough St., and used regularly for Football Specials taking dockyardees and matelots to Home Park.

The takeover also saw the Stonehouse company's green cars at once moved to Milehouse where some temporary tracks were laid, adjacent to Alma Road. The cars were then taken one by one into the depot for rebuilding and/or modification over a span of a couple of years. B.Y.Williams recalls: 'I only once saw a P.S.D. car still in green pressed into service for a football car, one Saturday afternoon from Fore Street to Home Park.' The fifteen Stonehouse cars became Nos. 113 - 127 in the Plymouth fleet. Ten, Nos. 114 - 123, were altered for use on circular routes only and carried the words 'Circular Route' emblazoned on the dashes. One end was fully vestibuled, for the driver; having its stairs removed and stairwell decked over. Two passenger seats were provided (for use at the driver's discretion) either side of the sliding door from the saloon, which was the only access to/from the platform. The platform at the conductor's end, with controls removed, except for the handbrake wheel, remained open. Four cars, Nos. 124 -127, were rebuilt normally but with stairs altered from reversed to direct. No. 113, formerly No. 16, the newest of the Stonehouse fleet, having always had direct stairs, was not altered, but may have been remotored. (In 1931, No. 119 of the circular route cars, was rebuilt as a double-ender.)

At this stage of the story, with the disappearance of both the Devonport and Stonehouse companies a *fait accompli*, it is perhaps appropriate to reflect on the parish pump politics which had preserved friction between the separate concerns and prevented Plymouth from ever developing a planned and cohesive tramway network. Strange though it may seem today, the saving in time and expense to the passenger of such a boundary-crossing system were scarcely considered. The respective corporations of Plymouth and Devonport believed that

Circular route car No.114 (ex-Stonehouse) in speckled brown livery, at the rear of Milehouse. Note the point in the overhead wiring and control to turn it which ran the post to a pull plunger.

Official PCT picture of ex-Stonehouse car 118 converted for circular route working with the front end vestibuled. Also displayed are Stokes' colourful route-indication boards below the windows.

it was in their interests to discourage through running, to keep trade within their own town. In the event, the amalgamation of the Three Towns and the subsequent introduction of through cars from the suburbs of Devonport to the centre of Plymouth spelt financial ruin to the large shopkeepers of Devonport, and many large shops went out of business or had to reduce their operations, whilst the Plymouth shops flourished. Ironically, the Plymouth Corporation had always been the most bitterly opposed to through running, and the Devonport company most persistent in trying to introduce it.

As shown by the accompanying small map, the geography of the Three Towns was such that by keeping services within borough boundaries, some of the routes were perforce absurdly devious. At unification the system was crying out for modernisation, but this involved raising capital which in the aftermath of war was not forthcoming.

Map of the Three Towns: This map overleaf of the conurbation of Plymouth, Devonport and Stonehouse shows how short-sighted was the policy of the municipalities to keep their tram services within their own borders. What was needed was a jointly-planned system giving the travelling public through running on direct routes to all areas, and readily capable of expansion as population grew and the northern and eastern boundaries receded.

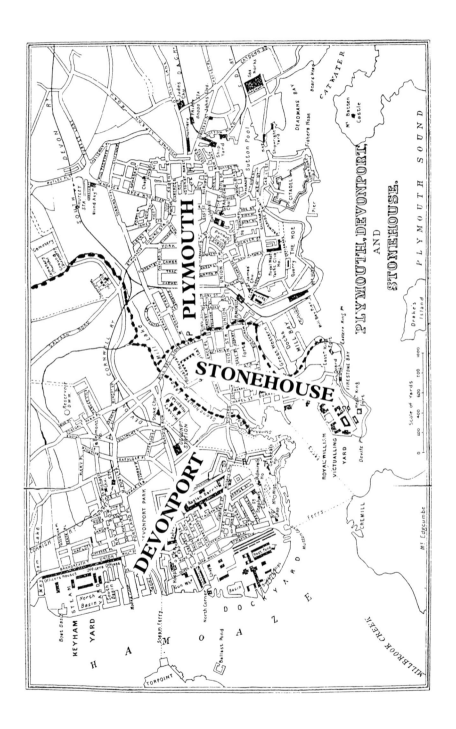

50

7

ELECTRIC TRAMS
PLYMOUTH CORPORATION: 1901 — 1918

The two electric routes operating in 1901 were augmented by a third the following year, when the route to Beaumont Road was opened on 2 April, 1902, with a terminus at Jephson Road. (Twenty years later the service was extended a sixth of a mile to terminate at Heathfield Road, just beyond the Mount Gold Fever hospital, to serve the Astor Trust houses and Council housing estates.)

On 2 June 1902, Plymouth suffered perhaps its worst-ever peacetime fire when Spooner's departmental store in Old Town Street went up in flames. The road became impassable between East Street and St. Andrew's Cross and tram services had to be suspended. So great was the heat that some tram-wire standards were distorted, bringing down the overhead wires.

Another ten tramcars were acquired in 1903. A first batch of six, numbered 21 - 26, were balconied Milnes cars with four side-windows, on Peckham cantilever trucks. All were fitted with the now standard handwheel-operated track brakes. A second batch of four, numbered 27 - 30 had similar bodies but on Brush Conalty trucks and with Westinghouse controls. Both batches had direct stairs, which - for right-handed people — were undoubtedly safer.

From 1903/4 redevelopment was taking place at the junction of Old Town Street, Ebrington Street and Market Avenue, to create the road junction of Drake Circus - which today survives only as a pedestrian precinct. This involved re-alignment of tram tracks, and at the same time the Tramways administration offices were moved from Market Avenue to No 15 Ebrington Street, where they remained till 1923. The Tramways Department soon had its own private telephone system, linking the administrative offices with the depots at Compton and Prince Rock and various call boxes located at track junctions for the use

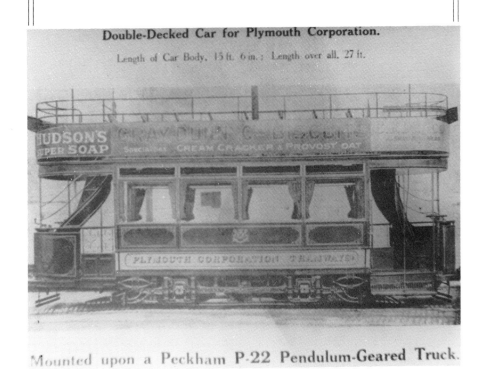

Double-Decked Car for Plymouth Corporation.

Length of Car Body, 15 ft. 6 in. ; Length over all, 27 ft.

Mounted upon a Peckham P-22 Pendulum-Geared Truck.

A car of the 21-30 series in original condition, mounted on a Peckham P22 Pendulum-Geared Truck. A number of these cars had long-wheelbase trucks, but their axles were given a limited swivelling freedom, to ease the passage aound curves. Length of car body: 15'6"; length overall: 27 feet. Seen here in the bright red, elaborately lined livery, and window side-curtains. (Photo — PCT)

Prior to 1906 and the completion of Drake Circus, cars for Compton and Peverell used the narrow northern part of Old Town Street. In this postcard picture a 7-20 series car, bound for Peverell, is entering the single line of this section of Old Town Street. Subsequently a short length of this track remained as a spur.

of tram crews.

The Peverell route from Hyde Park Corner to Peverell Park Corner was electrified in 1905, opening on January 13. Local politics saw to it that no connection was made with the Devonport company's Tor Lane - Fore Street tracks, which passed only a few tantalising yards from the Peverell terminus. Over the years a number of approaches were made to the Plymouth Corporation by the Devonport company for link-ups and through running at Peverell, Fore Street and Pennycomequick but says Sambourne 'at every attempt the tramway committee adopted a hostile attitude.'

In the same year six new cars arrived, numbers 31 - 36. They were Brush-built balconied cars with three side-windows and direct stairs, described by Gentry as 'a considerable advance on previous types': an intriguing comment since they were still open-topped, unvestibuled and with wooden seating. However they were the first of the three large windows-a-side cars and in general were almost standard with later cars supplied by Brush. All except No. 34, withdrawn in 1924, gave nearly thirty years service. They were fitted with framed roller-blind indicators showing the destination in white letters on a black field.

The 21st September 1905 saw the electrification of the line to Pen-nycomequick, which diverged from the Compton route at the Harvest Home, and utilised the former horse and steam tram tracks in Coburg Street. At Plymouth North Road station, where Saltash Road had an incline of 1 in 9, the ascending line (only) had a spur into the station approach. This was convenient for baggage-encumbered train passengers boarding trams for the town centre, but the arrangement was short-lived. Additional brakes were at first fitted to cars using Saltash Road hill, but these were later deemed unnecessary, and were removed.

It was at last the turn of the West Hoe line to be electrified, and in 1906 the Brush Company supplied six single-deckers (officially, demi-cars) to work it. Small cars, they measured 21'10" long over fenders, with an 11'4" body, and were mounted on 5'6" wheelbase trucks. Their half-enclosed end-platforms were designed for one man operation, passengers boarding at the front near-side, and paying the driver. Seating for three was provided on both platforms, and in good weather the seats at the driver's end were popular with the public. The short wheelbase caused these trams to pitch badly in motion, and the very long trolley arm frequently left the overhead wire. A long, crook'd bamboo pole was provided to enable the driver to pull down the bobbing arm and jockey it back under the wire, to the accompaniment of blue sparks and minor pyrotechnics. The electric service began on 22 June, 1907, and the single-deckers ran between the Hoe and Pennycomequick, until the link-up with the Devonport lines, 1915 - 16. When the through services commenced, the North Road spur was disconnected, and later lifted. At the West Hoe end the line was extended eastwards at electrification to a terminus just beyond the Promenade Pier, the former terminal spur in Pier Street being lifted. The old steam and horse tram depot at Millbay was not electrified, but closed down and sold, becoming Tuckett's sweet factory. Subsequently a single car ran a shuttle service between the Pier and a short spur laid in at Drake Circus.

The demi-cars were latterly used for relief duties at times of pressure on the Prince Rock and Beaumont Road routes. B. Y. Williams recalls riding on one in Ebrington Street *c.* 1920. The original Route 9 was closed in 1921 and other services — frequently No. 5 — were extended to serve West Hoe as required. The single-deckers then lay for three years disused at Milehouse.

In 1913 permission was sought from the Board of Trade to run covered-top double-deckers in Plymouth, but the request was turned down. In fact, none of the twelve tramway systems in the south-west, from Worcester or Swindon to Camborne, ever ran a covered-top car.

When the Great War broke out in 1914, the Corporation tram routes, now all electrified, were as follows:

Theatre — Compton;
Theatre — Peverell;
West Hoe — North Road Station;
Theatre — Beaumont Road;
Theatre — Prince Rock.

Although route destinations were shown on the roller-blinds, these services were not at first numbered on the cars themselves; route indication for the illiterate taking the form of coloured discs hung on car dashboards above the fleet number. Colours of discs were as follows:

Compton — Vertical blue & white halves
Peverell — Plain white
West Hoe — (none carried)
Beaumont Road — White circle, green border
Prince Rock — Red star on white circle

Similar coloured lights were displayed on the bulkhead at night.
Minimum fares were ¹/₂d, full distance on all routes, 1¹/₂d; but a universal penny fare replaced this tariff for the early war years. As tram crews were gradually absorbed into the Forces, women took their places, and peak-capped, long-skirted conductresses were soon punching tickets and handling recalcitrant trolley arms with the same nonchalance as the men.

The year 1914 brought not only war, in August, but the union of the Three Towns in October; and the latter had the more immediate impact on the tramway scene. Plymouth Corporation bought out the Devonport company, taking over its rolling stock and depots. Absorption and integration were inhibited by wartime shortages and restrictions, so for the duration the Devonport services were run as a separate concern. But by mid-October, 1915, track connections were being made at Peverell and Pennycomequick, some through running commenced, and Corporation trams were regularly being stabled at Milehouse. Of the thirty-three Devonport cars, seven were deemed unfit for further service, and stored: the remaining twenty-six being eventually numbered 63 - 88 in the Plymouth fleet. Of these, fifteen were original Brill cars. B.Y.Williams recalls: 'There was a gold and blue transfer label inside each American-built car, affixed by Brill. In later years the varnished woodwork inside the cars was painted over white and the transfers thus were hidden.' The new through services were numbered as follows:

1	Theatre — Compton;
2	Theatre — Fore Street *via* Peverell;
3	Theatre — Morice Square *via* Peverell;
4	Theatre — Beaumont Road;
5	Theatre — Prince Rock;
6	Guildhall — Fore Street *via* Stuart Road;
7	Guildhall — St. Budeaux *via* Stuart Road;
8	Morice Squre — St. Budeaux;
9	Drake Circus — West Hoe (but number not carried on cars).

White discs with black numbers were hung on the dash. Later, black discs were used with route numbers in white.

The St. Budeaux - Saltash Passage line was closed for the duration, and a double spur was laid in by St. Andrew's tower as a terminus for Routes 6 and 7 designated 'Guildhall'. Meanwhile, the Corporation had acquired twelve new cars. These came from the Brush Company, with Peckham P22 trucks. They were balconied, with direct stairs, and numbered 43 - 54. (Of these, no. 45 was destined after the war to be fitted with experimental leather seats in the lower saloon.) Sambourne records the acquisition, in 1915, of a canvas-sided railgrinder; but although the need for one at a time when new rail was virtually unobtainable seems evident, we have been unable to confirm that the system possessed one before 1922.

With traffic intensified due to the large numbers of servicemen in Plymouth, and the Dockyard labour force up to 15,837, the Corporation managed to acquire another six cars before the end of the war. Four three-windowed, balconied Brush cars on Peckham P22 trucks, numbered 55 - 58 arrived in 1916, and two more of the same design, numbered 60 and 61, in 1917. In a Tramway Review (Summer 1980) article, K. H. Rutherford recalls watching the arrival of some of this 55 class, by LSWR goods train; and after the war - of the delivery of the 94 - 105 class, which followed them, by the G.W.R.

By the end of the war the Plymouth tramway system could be described as 'the worse for wear'. The absence of young fit staff in the Services, and wartime shortage of track work and wiring had combined to make maintenance and renewals a constant problem. Recovery from this run-down state was clearly a first priority when peace should come.

Meanwhile in 1915 the Corporation had obtained powers to operate motor buses; not, at the time, with the remotest view of their rivalling the tram system, but to give the Tramways Department flexibility in countering the competition of private bus and coach concerns, and to act as feeders to tram termini. Nevertheless, to the far-sighted it was a cloud, if a distant one, on the horizon of the tramways. War conditions however prevented the Corporation from obtaining suitable vehicles and the matter was set aside for the duration.

The ill-fated Compton-built rail grinder.

8

ELECTRIC TRAMS
PLYMOUTH CORPORATION: 1918 - 1922

With the end of hostilities the General Manager, C.R.Everson, retired, and in his place was appointed H.P.Stokes, formerly General Manager of the Bexley & Dartford Tramway and Electricity Department in Kent. He started at once on a comprehensive programme of reorganisation, stock repair, and general refurbishment of track, standards and over-head wiring.

Centralisation at Milehouse, the former Devonport company's depot, seems to have been Stokes' priority. Over a period of four years, Compton was run down to a tram storage depot, and the workshop machinery and equipment from its 1901 overhaul works were trans-ferred to Milehouse to augment the ex-Devonport equipment, and installed in the original tramsheds. Before losing its workshop, Comp-ton built a rail-grinder, designed by H.P.Stokes and his assistant J.W.Eunion. The main truck of the grinder carried a 25 h.p. electric motor and all operating gear for travelling and feed of the machine. The grinding attachment had two 18" diameter grinding wheels, powered via the overhead trolley wire, and these ground level the hammered railjoints where built up by the electric welder. When fast travelling the machine had a variable speed on any gradient of 7 to 15m.p.h.; and when grinding, a reversible feed of fifteen feet per minute. A proud Department euphemistically described it as 'very silent in operation and only noticeable by the shower of sparks from the grinding wheels.' It was fated one day in the 'twenties to run out of control at Drake Circus, crashing into Holmes' furniture shop in Old Town Street and, sadly, killing the driver. Meanwhile, two new tramsheds, with three roads each, were built end-on to the east of the old sheds between 1921 and 1923 and a new entrance made at the Milehouse crossroads. Prince Rock was retained as a sub-depot, and Camel's Head for the temporary

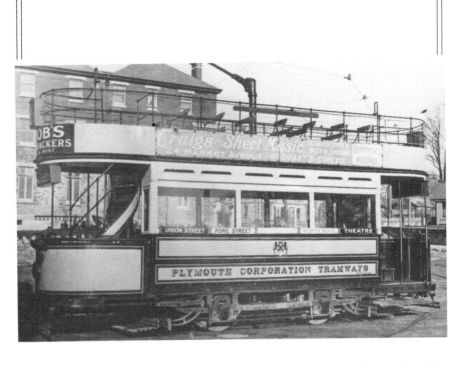

Tram No. 74, rebuilt from a Devonport Brill car of which little remains! The central body is the Brill's, but all else is new material, including truck and electrical equipment. (Photo — PCT official picture)

Tram No. 91, the first car that PCT claimed to have built. It has a Brill truck, probably from a dismantled Devonport car, but lengthened wheelbase. Seen here at Theatre, below Derry's Clock, c. 1932. (Photo — M.Bright)

storage of defective cars awaiting repair.

During 1919 and 1920 tram construction was undertaken at Milehouse for the first time, although the maximum use was made of old components. The seven ex-Devonport cars (five of them Brills) which had been found unfit for use had been stored since 1914 and were now cannibalised to assist the building of virtually new cars and the repair of others. Loss of information with the passage of time makes it precarious now to be definite about the rolling stock changes of this time; but Sambourne tells us, in summary, that twenty-eight cars were completely overhauled, sixteen bodies and twenty trucks rebuilt, and eight other bodies strengthened or extensively repaired; while he attributes three new cars, numbers 91, 93 and 112, to PCT construction. Ex-Devonport cars 74 and 83 were rebuilt with full top decks over canopies, though 83 was later reduced to a works car. No. 79 was cut down to a single-deck and converted to a breakdown/tow car. Nos. 90 and 92 were new cars supplied by Brush. They were balconied three-window cars with direct stairs on Peckham P22 trucks. Nos. 91 and 112 were virtually new cars, though 91 was basically a rebuilding of ex-Devonport 22; and No. 93 was a rebuild of ex-Devonport 24. All except 93, whose Devonport origin remained more obvious, were rebuilt to be generally similar to the Brush 55 - 58 class. No. 91 was first put to work on Route 3 and the PCT saw to it that the advent of this 'home-made' car received due publicity. As built the width of the top deck, rail to rail, was stretched to the limits and 2 x 2 seating was provided - except 1 x 1 by the trolley pole. The narrowed gangway however proved inconvenient, and the seating was soon altered to 2 x 1. The Brush company supplied another twelve cars in 1919, similar to 90 and 92, and numbered 94 to 105. A further two cars (to have been nos. 106 and 107) which had been ordered were for some reason sold instead to Exeter Corporation, where they became Nos. 26 and 27. This 'hiccup' is unexplained in books written nearer to the event. Probably Plymouth in an afterthought, wished to cancel two of their order, and the intervention of Exeter with an immediate need made this possible, but speculation seems idle. (However it looked as though fate would not be denied when these two cars, after eleven years service in Exeter, were included in a batch of nine redundant Exeter cars purchased cheaply by Plymouth in 1931.) The numbers 106 to 111 were left blank by the entry into service of No. 112 (newly built by Milehouse) and in fact were to remain unused. In a remarkably short space of time, considering the difficulties of immediate post-war years, H.P.Stokes had

Ex-Devonport BRILL car as Plymouth No. 79, cut down for Works purposes, and painted dark green. Adjacent, left, is Plymouth car No. 91, built at Milehouse but incorporating truck from a dismantled Brill. (Photo — B. Y. Williams)

Ex-Devonport BRILL car, as Plymouth No. 76, after renovation and remotoring c. 1920. Here photographed at Milehouse on the way to Fore Street to return as a football special, c. 1929. (Photo — B. Y. Williams)

rejuvenated the Plymouth tramways fleet, and was making Milehouse a thriving transport centre.

Out on the tracks there was also much evidence of the new broom. The overhead-wire standards received their first coat of paint for fourteen years and new track replaced much that had deteriorated. Single track was doubled in Hyde Park Road (Routes 2 & 3), Milehouse Road (Routes 2 & 3) and St. Levan Road (Routes 3 & 10). A three-track layout was installed in the narrow confines of Basket Street to provide the 6 & 7 Routes with a new terminus, and the 'Guildhall' double spur by St. Andrew's tower was then lifted. At Drake Circus a curve was laid in Ebrington Street northbound to Tavistock Road. Used sometimes for cars going to and from H.M.Dockyard, this link never formed part of a regular service route. In Fore Street, the terminal spur abandoned in 1901 was reinstated as a looped siding for football cars to Home Park. When the Dockyard worked on Saturday mornings, Argyle home matches — alone in the Football league — used to start at 3.15 p.m. instead of 3 p.m. to give time for the tramloads of dockyardees to reach the ground. In 1921 Route 9 to West Hoe was withdrawn and the service provided by extending Routes 4 or 5 to Hoe and Piers as required. As from 1922 the junction layout at Theatre was more complex (*see* diagrams of interchange points). The main points were controlled from a wooden box in which there was a single horizontal lever which moved in several slots.

But by far the most important innovation was the laying down of the Alma Road route from a junction with existing tracks at Pennycomequick to the junction at Milehouse. Work on this line, which opened for through traffic in May 1922, had been pushed forward to be ready for the start of the Bath and West agricultural show on June 1st, on a site which is now part of Central Park. As events turned out, this was to be the last tram route laid down in Plymouth.

Fares meanwhile had been revised. The wartime universal 1d fare was no longer appropriate after 1916 when longer routes resulted from the link-up with the Devonport lines. Each route was now divided into penny stages, but three stages could be travelled for 1½d and 4 stages for 2d. Thereafter stages cost ½d extra to a maximum of 4d for a full journey; but later, Routes 7 and 14 cost 5d over the full distance. Nevertheless, Plymouth tram fares had always been, and continued to be too low to provide adequate renewal funds; quite apart from repayment of the original loans which funded the installation of the system, and were known as the 'Tramway Debt'.

One of Stokes' innovations which lasted only a few years was a system of narrow coloured boards (enamelled iron plated on wood), indicating districts served en route, which were carried in a row in slots under the side windows. Examples were: Friary, black letters on green board; Mutley, red on white; Peverell, white on red; Stoke, white on blue; Theatre, white on black. A single similar board, giving destination only, was displayed either end, on the dash, over the fleet number, as the discs had been. These end boards were always superfluous, as the roller-blind indicators above them were large and clear. The side-window boards were probably useful to visitors to Plymouth, and looked well when they were newly painted. But the requisite slots were not provided on trams built after 1924 and thereafter the use of the boards lapsed.

1922 was arguably the most significant year in the history of Plymouth tramways since electrification. Five new services were opened, the first two resulting directly from the laying down of the Alma Road track. These were:

9   (Circular) Theatre to Milehouse via Mutley Plain and Peverell, returning via Alma Road;

9A   (same route in reverse direction);

10   Theatre to Morice Square, via Alma Road and North Keyham.

Route 9/9A proved unprofitable and was short-lived. Within months it had been cut to a Basket Street - Peverell to and fro service, and given the letter P in lieu of its number.

Two other routes were simply takeovers, with extensions, of the former Stonehouse company's route, Plymouth's original tramway:

11   Beaumont Road to Fore Street, *via* Theatre & Union Street;

12   Prince Rock to Fore Street, *via* Theatre & Union Street.

Meanwhile connections laid in at Fore Street between the former Devonport and Stonehouse companies' tracks enabled Routes 2 and 6 to become circular, and they now returned to Theatre via the Stonehouse tracks. Cars in the reverse direction bore the same numbers, but were designated 2A and 6A for administrative purposes, and this applied also to 9A. The number 13 was studiously avoided, but one further service was added in the November:

14   Theatre to St. Budeaux *via* Milehouse and Albert Road.

Route 14's former Devonport company's track from St. Budeaux on to Saltash Passage had been disused for eight years. Ex-Plymothian Michael Gardner of Dublin, was later (1964) to write to *The Western Evening Herald* of his memories of the route in those days: 'The very first time on which I made the journey (in 1922), St. Budeaux was the terminus. The lines continued, rusted and clogged, but no tram ever ran on them.'

Also in 1922 came a change of livery. The vermilion and gold which had obtained since 1892 was abandoned in favour of primrose yellow and white with broad red lining on the yellow panels. The change was also a break with tradition, as Plymouth trams had been red since 1885. The last car to be painted in the red livery was No. 113, ex-Stonehouse 'green car' No. 16, reconditioned. The first car to appear in the yellow livery was No. 116, ex-Stonehouse 12.

Meanwhile the Corporation had been able to implement their powers to operate motor buses. It was on 14 July 1920, that the first bus service commenced running in Plymouth. Twenty Straker-Square single-deck twenty-four seaters, running on solid tyres, had been acquired by the Corporation to work four bus routes. They were finished in the same red-lined primrose livery as the trams, and were derisively nicknamed 'the yellow perils' and the 'boneshakers'; but that small, distant cloud on the tramway horizon had now drawn much nearer.

Tram No.57 at Hoe and Piers terminus in the summer of 1923, whilst on Route 9. This followed a serpentine course which nearly completed a circuit — Pier, Pennycomequick, Milehouse, Peverell, Mutley, and back to Pier; also vice-versa: but only ran thus for a short period. (Photo — B. Y. Williams)

9

THE YEARS OF GROWTH: 1923 - 1928

The policy of concentrating the Tramways Department on Milehouse was carried a significant step forward in 1923 when the imposing redbrick administration offices were opened there, facing Milehouse Road. Still bearing the legend 'Plymouth Corporation Tramways', it is today the headquarters of Plymouth Citybus Limited. Meanwhile the Market Street depot of the former Stonehouse company's trams was sold, and has since become a tyre warehouse. The tram tracks and traverser are still *in situ*, but the pits have been filled in and all are buried under asphalt. The building now stands alone on a site otherwise cleared for redevelopment, so its days are probably numbered.

In July 1923 the track from St. Budeaux to Saltash Passage was put in order, and Route 14 cars thereafter ran through to the ferry. This was surely the most romantic of Plymouth tram termini, with the broad sweep of Tamar alongside, and the lofty spans of Brunel's railway bridge overhead. The terminus had, remarkably, a scissors crossing, though one arm was rarely if ever used. During summer afternoons Route 14 was also extended at its other end to Hoe and Piers; and was then, at nine miles, Plymouth's longest tram ride.

The Corporation trams were now operating thirteen routes, a number that was never exceeded. These, with their full-distance fares, were as follows:

1   Theatre and Compton; Single fare: 1½d;
2   Circular: Theatre - Peverell - Fore Street and *vice-versa*: 4d;
3   Theatre and Morice Square *via* Peverell: 3d;
4   West Hoe/Millbay and Beaumont Road: 2d/1½d;
5   West Hoe/Millbay and Prince Rock: 2d/1½d;
6   Circular: Theatre, P'quick, Fore Street and *vice-versa:* 3d;
7   Theatre and St. Budeaux, *via* Wilton Street: 3d single and Keyham 5d return;

Milehouse Works in the mid-'twenties. Note new tramsheds built end-on to the original Devonport buildings. Note the site of an old leat, being cleared for housebuilding. Halfway down the hill trees mark the course of the Dockyard leat.

8   Morice Square and St. Budeaux: 1½d;
9   Theatre - Theatre, *via* Peverell and P'quick (*not* circular): 3d;
10   Theatre and Morice Square, *via* Pennycomequick: 2d;
11   Beaumont Road and Fore Street, *via* Theatre: 3d single, 5d return;
12   Prince Rock and Fore Street, *via* Theatre: 3d single, 5d return;
14   Theatre and Saltash Passage, *via* Pennycomequick, Milehouse, Keyham, St. Budeaux: 4d single, 6d return.

Manager Stokes is said to have argued for a long distance extension over Roborough Down to Yelverton and Tavistock but there seems no evidence that the Tramways Committee seriously considered it.

In 1923 or '24 - we have been unable to verify the date — a tower lorry used for repair of the overhead wires ran out of control while descending Tavistock Road, near the Public Library. Fearing a multiple collision at Drake Circus, the driver endeavoured valiantly to turn around after passing Spear's Corner and crashed into the window of a footwear shop. The lorry lost its tower and there were some injured, including the driver, but no fatalities.

The year 1924 was marked chiefly by changes in rolling stock. The six 'demi-car' single-deckers formerly employed on the West Hoe route, and which had lain disused for several years, were all, except No. 42, broken up. No. 42 was converted to a welding car, and on this account was fated to become the longest-surviving Plymouth tram when the end came. In its new guise No. 42 had a 47 hp shunt motor and generator direct coupled, mounted on a bedplate with two grid-type resistances and the required control switches. The generator gave a normal output of 60 volts at 500 amps. By day this welding car was in continuous use on such repairs as truck frames, gear cases, motor cases and armature shafts; while at night it worked on the welding of fishplates, bonds and the building up of hammered joints on the track. Repainted dark green, no. 42 suffered the indignity of losing its number, which was bestowed on an ex-Devonport car in a renumbering muddle.

Also in 1924 too, twenty new cars were obtained from the English Electric Company (formerly Dick Kerr Limited) and were the first fully-vestibuled cars to run in Plymouth. Nos. 131 - 150 were also larger and of higher capacity than their predecessors, and their platforms having an angled, instead of rounded dash, they were quickly dubbed

Works cars at Milehouse: left —a Brill stripped of passenger fittings and used for depot and towing purposes. Right — the erstwhile demi-car No. 42, fitted for welding purposes for laying the new Alma Road lines and subsequent welding duties elsewhere.

E.E.C. "Squareface" No. 137 in yellow livery at the rear of Milehouse sheds. (Photo — B. Y. Williams)

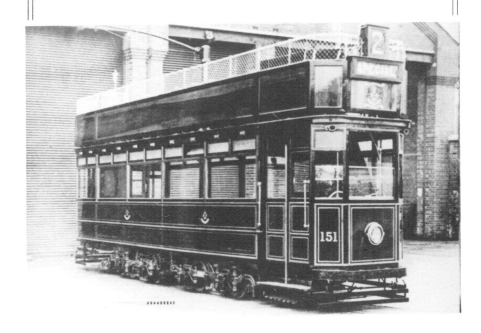

*The first of the Stokes' bogie cars to be turned out by Milehouse Works —
No.151. This is the official PCT photograph of the car in its original teak
finish. Alone of the class, No.151 carried a large central headlamp on the
dash. Note the two Plymouth crests on waist panel, one over each bogie.*

No. 151 as subsequently altered: (1) Bogies replaced by 4-wheel truck (the bogies had given a jerky ride and there had been derailments); (2) Platform doors removed; (3) Route number box removed; (4) Repainted in maroon and cream livery, with single, central coat of arms on waist panel.

'the squarefaces' by the crews. All were turned out with the Spartan wooden seating to which Plymothians had long become resigned, but most of the twenty were later given traverse, leather-upholstered seats downstairs. An innovation with Nos. 131 - 150 was that their end platforms were built as a unit with the body; — this overcame the tendency to platform 'droop' observed with some of their predecessors. There was no step between platform and saloon — the whole unit was lower with smaller wheels and improved modern, smaller, motors. With three exceptions, the class were broken up in 1938, but Nos. 142 - 4 survived long enough to suffer damage in Hitler's war, and be broken up in 1942. Why the class were numbered from 131 is unexplained. It left numbers 128 to 130 unused, and so they remained. There was a considerable 'slaughter' of the oldest trams in 1924, including all the original Milnes cars except No. 1.

With the addition of the Compton works machinery, Milehouse now had comprehensive workshops. The foundry output was approximately eight tons of iron castings and two tons of non-ferrous metal per week. A lathe installed in 1925 could deal expeditiously with wheel centres and tyres. A 25 h.p. variable speed motor drove the lathe. A pair of standard 32" diameter wheels could be machined in less than half an hour.

By 1925 it was clear that the tram fleet would have to be further augmented to meet traffic requirements. Milehouse engineering staff and equipment being now capable of the task, General Manager Stokes determined to design and build the required trams himself. It was decided to begin with a prototype and build another fifteen if the first was successful in service. The construction of this new, high-capacity bogie tram was the highlight of 1925. The body was fashioned in solid teak and was given upholstered seating on both decks, although the saloon seating remained longitudinal. Even the bogies were built at Milehouse. The car had compressed-air bells and platform doors, the motors and all electrical equipment being supplied by E.E.C. Limited, including the magnetic braking system. But ... the car was still an open-topper. A (repeat) request to the Board of Trade to sanction covered-top cars had again been refused, the reason given being Plymouth's narrow-gauge track, severe curves and steep gradients. Since these conditions obtained at other places which had been allowed covered-top cars, it seems the Board of Trade was less than frank in its answer. Perhaps its inspectors had reported unfavourably on the condition of the Plymouth track, for the standard of maintenance was admittedly not high.

When completed, car No. 151 was finished in teak varnish with gold lining, which made her a one-off in a fleet which was currently changing from red-lined primrose yellow to unlined daffodil yellow and white with black lettering! She was taken for extensive trials on circular Route 2, and these proved conspicuously successful except for the negotiation of sharp curves. Outside the Repertory Theatre in Princess Square car No.151 derailed time and again, with much delay to traffic during re-railing. She returned to Milehouse workshops for modification to the bogies, and the opportunity was taken to fit her with an additional air-braking system before return to traffic.

Thereafter the construction of the other fifteen cars went ahead, Nos. 152 - 166 being completed over the following two and a half years and all being fitted with both air and magnetic brakes. No. 166 was destined to be the highest-numbered car on the system. The bogies, despite modification, were never really satisfactory on this class, and before long the wood-block road surface at Princess Square corner was badly scored by these cars de-railing. Eventually, between 1930 and 35 all the class except three (Nos. 156, 163 and 164) were converted to long-wheelbase single-truck vehicles, which gave them a dangerous overhang on curves. The teak varnish finish was continued, and earned the cars the nickname of 'Brown Bears' by the crews. No. 151 was distinguishable from the rest of the class in having the roller-blind destination frames placed higher, and a single central dashlight whereas the remainder had twin head and tail lamps. During 1925 only one Plymouth tramcar was reported scrapped. This was No. 70, the former Devonport company's Birmingham No. 30.

The General Strike, lasting nine days from May 4th to 12th, marked the year 1926. In Plymouth, although all buses were confined to their garages, a limited service of trams continued to operate. On the 4th of May only three tram men turned up for work at Milehouse, and one at Prince Rock. On the 8th a letter from Manager Stokes was sent to every driver and conductor urging a return to work; and a skeleton service was kept running with a few regular crews and a number of hurriedly instructed volunteers. Your author Martin Langley, who travelled to school by tram, well remembers the boarded-up side windows, barbed wire around the dashes, and wire netting protecting the drivers in the unvestibuled cars. On May 9th there were two attacks on trams by a rowdy element in Old Town Street. In the first instance the route indication boards were pulled from their slots and used to break the

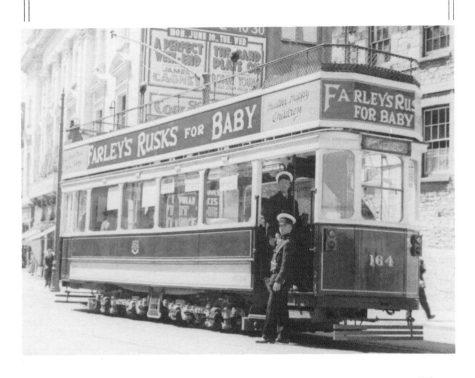

No. 164 mounted on original bogies at Devonport terminus, c. 1932. (Photo — B. Y. Williams)

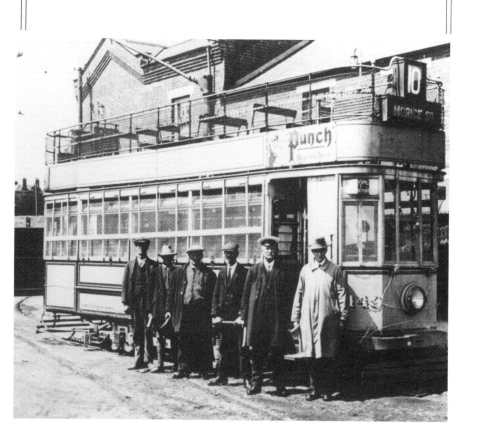

The General Strike of 1926 caused suspension of services at first, but then some limited trips were run. Intimidation of drivers and stone-throwing led to another brief suspension. Some cars, as 'square-face' 149 shown here, were then 'armoured' and ran on Route 2 without further incident.

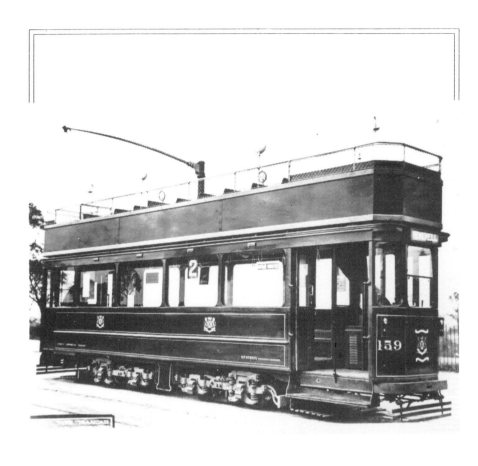

PCT official photograph of No. 159 as built, in varnished teak all over. Note Plymouth coat-of-arms placed centrally on the dash, and combined head-lamp/rear light units on either side.

No.159 as later altered. The dashboard coat-of-arms has been replaced by the car number. Shown in Jackson's maroon livery which included creamy-white rocker panel.

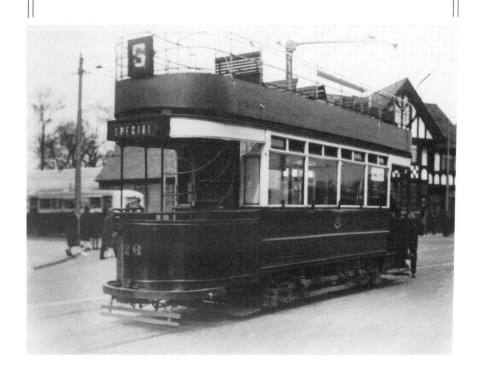

Car No. 26 of the 21-30 class at Milehouse crossroads, with the Britannia Inn in the background. About 1929, in speckeld brown livery. Note modifications: dash sheeting continuous to car side panels; route-number boxes; altered toplights to windows. (Photo — B.Y.Williams)

side-windows. Police drew their batons and arrested two men. Later that day two drivers, one elderly, were dragged from their platforms and received medical treatment after rough handling. Two men and a woman were arrested. Unknown probably to most of the public, the drivers were thereafter issued with truncheons for self-defence. At least one of these truncheons, now engraved 'Plymouth Corporation Tramways. General Strike, 1926', is still preserved by the family of the late H.P.Stokes.

A derailment akin to that of June 1902 (i.e. a blocked rail groove) occurred about 1927 which fortunately did not have disastrous consequences. Philip Liddicoat (organist of St. Andrews in succession to Dr.H.Moreton (*see* footnote in Chapter 8) was a passenger, with his father, in one of the 70-series cars when the mishap occurred. The car was at the junction of Exmouth Road and Albert Road when the Points Boy employed there at busy periods dropped his bar lever in the rail groove. The car lurched off the track but did not turn over nor hit another vehicle.

This incident was close to what was arguably the most dangerous spot on the system, — where Portland Road runs from Exmouth Road beside Devonport Park toward the river. The northbound track at this point was perched on the brink of the steep hill; and had a derailment occurred here the results could have been serious indeed. In token there was a notice board fixed to the park railings: 'ALL CARS MUST PROCEED AT A DEAD SLOW RATE PAST THIS POINT'.

In 1927 a third new tram shed, with three roads, was erected at Milehouse, adjacent to the sheds built in 1921 and 23. Meanwhile the building of the 151 class trams continued into 1928. Not wishing to paint over their varnished exteriors, the General Manager decided to bring the rest of the fleet into line by painting all other cars a speckled brown with white upperworks, gold lining and small gold lettering. It was not a happy choice. The black-flecked deep brown neither blended with the teak-varnished cars, nor looked pleasing in its own right, and was destined to be short-lived. Since the changeover from red-lined primrose yellow to unlined daffodil yellow was still in progress, the tram fleet was now acquiring a harlequin appearance. In 1928, the year in which Plymouth achieved city status, the tramway system reached its apogee, with 127 cars working 17$\frac{1}{2}$ miles of route.

Although tramcar liveries in Plymouth are said to have changed more often than in any other city, the uniform of the crews under Corporation management remained constant. Every driver and con-

Plymouth Corporation Nos.118, 142, 127 at Milehouse. Note No.118 converted for use on circular route only. (Photo — B.Y.Williams)

ductor was issued annually with a navy-blue red-piped suit, greatcoat and peaked cap with white cover for summer. The caps bore nickel badges denoting 'Motorman' or 'Conductor' in longhand lettering. Oilskins and waterproof aprons were provided in bad weather for men driving unvestibuled cars. When cared for, this uniform was quite smart. In contrast to the laissez-faire attitude common today toward wearing of uniforms, it enhanced the public image of the service. Comic hats sported by some drivers during a mid-twenties Plymouth Carnival Week were quickly given the thumbs-down by the Manager.

The same period of the latter 'twenties which saw the high-water mark of the tramway system witnessed also the inexorable advance of the motor bus. The first pneumatic-tyred buses were on Plymouth streets in 1925, and by 1927 the Corporation had seventy-two buses including twenty-five AECs with Milehouse-built, teak-varnished bodies. By March 1928 ten bus routes were being operated, albeit by single-deck 20 - 26 seaters. From 1925 to 1930 a Cattedown - West Hoe service was worked by six Shelvoke and Drewry small-wheelers, soon nicknamed 'the caterpillars' by the public. It was becoming evident that for the trams, the writing was on the wall.

A 'thirties picture of car No.151 (the original 'brown bear') at Theatre terminus, in Jackson's maroon livery and after substitution of a four-wheeled truck in place of the original two bogies. Note that the car has drawn up with the boarding platform opposite the railed queue-gangway.

10

THE YEARS OF DECLINE: 1929 - 1939

In 1929 H.P.Stokes retired after ten years at the helm, to be succeeded by Clement Jackson M.I.A.E., who had been manager of Oldham Corporation Transport in Lancashire. Reports suggest that he was somewhat taken aback on discovering that his new tramway system was sporting four different liveries — red-lined primrose yellow, unlined daffodil yellow, speckled brown, and teak varnish! Before the year was out he had introduced the colour scheme he had used at Oldham — a gold-lined maroon, with white lined in red; and within eighteen months all regular-use cars were in the new livery. The first car to appear in the new colours was No. 113, which, B.Y.Williams recalls, 'was given special treatment, with lampshades in the saloon!'

The working days of tram crews were sometimes not without incident. In the summer of 1929 a car was on the terminus spur at Hender's Corner, Compton, when a wretched schoolboy jumped on to the buffer and leant over the dash to release the brake. Fortunately no passengers were aboard, but the tram was on an incline and immediately started to move off. The conductor and motorman were twenty-five yards away, enjoying a smoke. They had to sprint fast, and they did. The miscreant scholar had meantime gone to ground. Justice certainly required that he be suitably punished, but prudence decreed that the less fuss the better, since the tram crew were grievously at fault in leaving the car unattended, and on a slope.

Since the demolition of the original 1899 Milnes cars nos. 2 - 6 five years previously, car No. 1 had been languishing behind the works at Milehouse. Alone of the group she had lasted long enough to receive the red-lined yellow livery and roller-blind route number boxes. She had been 'tarted up' for the Municipal Tramways Association Conference at Plymouth in June 1925, and then left in the yard to deteriorate.

Car No. 1 in eventual disuse at Milehouse depot, in yellow livery. It stood in a siding, gradually looking more weather-beaten, faded and forlorn — seen here c. 1928 or '29 — until one day it had gone the way of all old things! (Photo — B.Y. Williams)

Evidently sentiment did not rate highly with the new manager, for in 1929 she was quietly broken up. Today No. 1 would have been of immense interest, but Plymouth has many times been profligate with her historic relics and this was but another instance.

There were days when a tram-driver's life was not a happy one. Former conductor Ern Evans recalls an incident in 1930 on a Fore Street special, passing Mount Wise Cricket Ground. Motorman Harry Rowe, who was in his sixties, was suddenly drenched with regurgitated beer when a party of drunks on the top deck leant over his stairwell to vomit! Hastily he donned his cape, in time to receive another baptism, before pulling up at the next stop. In a militant mood he climbed the stairs and turned the miscreants off the tram. His young conductor was too helpless with laughter to assist.

The year 1930 saw a great slaughter of the old Devonport company trams which despite their immediate post-war refurbishment were now feeling their age. Twelve cars, Numbers 63 - 65, 77 - 78, 80 - 82 and 84 - 87 all succumbed to the cutter's torch before the year was out.

The new manager had come to his task at a crucial time. Very considerable expenditure was necessary if the tramway system was to meet the needs of increasing traffic and the housing suburbs. Not only would the route network have to be substantially extended, but whole-sale renewal of existing worn track and overhead wiring was essential, while thirteen tramcars were older even than the twelve ex-Devonport cars which he had condemned, and would have to be replaced. The alternatives were to convert the system to trolleybus operation or to abandon electric traction and develop the bus fleet. The Transport Committee asked him in the first instance to report on the practicability of converting tram Routes 4 and 5 to trolleybus working, which would in any case involve new wiring and road reinstatement through-out. After consideration of his report the Corporation decided to embark on a ten-year programme of phasing out the trams and replacement by double-decker buses, which is probably what Jackson himself favoured. The changeover was made gradual to allow for progressive reduction of the tramway debt. The loans outstanding on the initial construction of the tramways had hung about the neck of the system like a millstone, the annual excess of income over expenditure being regularly swallowed up by interest payments on the loans. Clement Jackson entered on a careful policy of make-do-and-mend, and in the following years was able to show an annual surplus while further reducing the debt. But the die had been cast, and the end of the

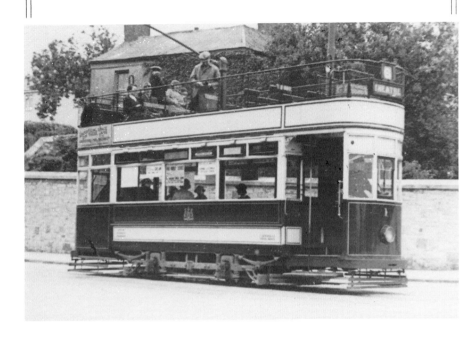

Ex-Exeter, renumbered PCT No. 1, eastbound on Route 6 at Pennycomequick. As can be seen, the ex-Exeters 1-7 had a shorter wheelbase than Plymouth cars, designed to negotiate a sharp curve in Exeter's Paris Street. (Photo — B. Y. Williams)

tramway system was in sight.

As early as October 1930 the breath of the new wind was evident when first, tram Route 8, and then the St. Budeaux - Saltash Passage section of Route 14, were closed and given over to buses; while Routes 7 and 14 were cut back to North Keyham — though later extended temporarily to R.N.Barracks. Meanwhile the Camel's Head depot was closed and sold, after the trams stored there had been removed to Milehouse. The depot became a garage-cum-petrol station, only to be demolished in 1973 when the area was redeveloped.

An essential part of Clement Jackson's modernisation plan was the phasing out, with the trams, of the single-decker buses, and their replacement by Leyland 'Titan' covered-top, double-deck, forty-eight seaters. Whereas tram travel compared favourably with that in the ricketty, single-deck buses hitherto employed, the Leyland Titans offered forty-eight upholstered seats under cover, smooth running and kerbside boarding. In 1931 a bus driver of your author's acquaintance averred that he had been overtaken by a tram in St. Levan Road when he was doing 30 m.p.h. in his Leyland. If this was indeed so, it seems that some motormen saw the buses as a challenge, and did not intend to yield pride of place meekly.

The delivery of ten further buses in 1931 made possible the closure of further tram routes, and services 4 (Beaumont Road - West Hoe), 5 (Prince Rock - Theatre) and 11 (Fore Street - Beaumont Road) were withdrawn. This meant that there were now more bus than tram routes operating under Corporation control.

One of the oldest remaining cars, Milnes No. 22 of 1903, was cleaned up and decorated for the 'All Electric House' exhibition in April 1931 and toured the city as a mobile display.

Replacement or costly renovation of some older cars had now become essential and this was met by the purchase of nine trams from Exeter Corporation, whose system was closing down that year. Seven of these cars (Exeter nos. 28 - 34, only six years old) were purchased for a total of £875; and two twelve-year-old cars (Exeter nos. 26 & 27), for only £75 each. These last two, by a quirk of fate, had actually been built for Plymouth by Brush in 1919, and bought by Exeter when Plymouth sought to cancel the order. They would then have been Plymouth nos. 106 and 107. Then open-ended, at Exeter they had since been vestibuled. Now the whole batch were numbered in a new series, 1 - 9. The ex-Exeters 1 - 7 were considered to be the fastest cars ever employed in Plymouth. For a few weeks in 1937, after buses should have taken over, they maintained the new, fast bus schedule for Route 6. A mechanic was in attendance at Pennycomequick to carry out minor tightening-up operations, such was the buffeting the cars suffered by being driven so hard in their old age!

It would seem that methodical numbering was anathema to the Tramways hierarchy. For no apparent reason, the Nos. 59, 62, 89, 108 - 111, 128 - 130 were never used; a muddle led to renumbering of nos. 71 and 73; some Milehouse Works cars carried numbers and some did not; and when the system was in the throes of closing, it was decided to start renumbering! Since the sum total of railed electric rolling stock ever owned was 176, there seems little excuse for such confusion.

During 1932 and '33 all but three of the ex-Stonehouse cars were broken up. The renovation in the early 'twenties does not alter the fact that most of them were over thirty years old: they had been good value for money.

On 11 April 1932, Route 1 to Compton was replaced by a bus service which ran to Hartley. Compton tram depot had for some years been used as a store for cars due for scrapping — although the better-conditioned among them had ventured out as Football Specials when Argyle was playing at home. As soon as these cars had been disposed of, the depot was sold (March 1933) to the Plymouth Transport Company (motto 'Anything - Anytime - Anywhere'), whose green and cream lorries used it until they were taken over by Drake Carriers Ltd. in 1963. When they moved out five years later elaborate plans were made for developing the 3½ acre site, but in 1973 a block of flats was agreed there to the designs of Marshman Warren and Taylor.

The Compton terminus had boasted a trolley arm reversing triangle to enable cars to reverse without the need for the conductor to lift the trolley off and walk it round. When the Compton line was closed this triangle was resited at the Prince Rock terminus.

No less than thirty-four redundant cars were cut up during 1934 and '35, including Milehouse's 'very own' 112, the last ten ex-Devonport cars, the last three ex-Stonehouse cars and — surprisingly — the unnumbered and ill-omened rail grinder.

There was also, however, a fresh intake. Twelve cars were purchased from Torquay, whose tram system had just closed down. Of these, six were long bogie-cars which gave none of the trouble of Plymouth's 151 class when cornering, but posed a fresh problem: their overhang was so great that they had to avoid meeting other cars on sharp curves! In accordance with the extraordinary 'Second Series' numbering, these

Ex-Torquay 'seasider' No.14 on Route 12 in the mid-'thirties. Photographed at the top of Chapel Street, Devonport. (Photo — B.Y.Williams)

Ex-Torquay bogie car numbered as PCT 15, eastbound on Route 12, passing Beaumont Park, Friary. The class proved best suited to this comparatively level route. (Photo — B.Y. Williams)

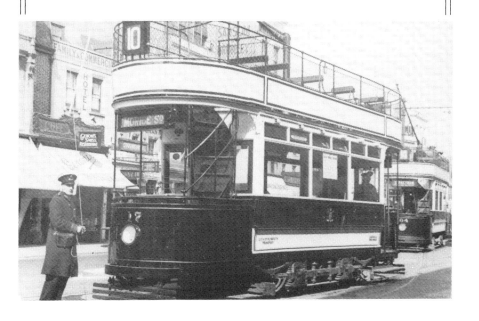

Ex-Torquay Brush-built 4-wheeler No.17 at rest outside Genoni's Cafe at Theatre terminus. The conductor has just swung the trolley arm round for the return journey. It has been suggested that this class of six cars was 'wished' on to Plymouth for a throw-away price. (Photo — B.Y.Williams)

trams - the largest to work on the Plymouth system - became nos. 10 to 15. The remaining six (Torquay nos. 7, 9 - 10, 16 - 18) were Brush-built four-wheelers and were principally used, numbered 16 - 21, on Dockyard Specials. We have been unable to discover what financial bargain Manager Jackson was able to strike for these 'seasiders'. Ex-Torquays 10 - 15 were splendid cars in motion, on the level. But they were hopelessly underpowered for hilly routes and were therefore confined to Route 12 till its closure, when they worked a while but not very successfully, on Route P. They were also deficient in braking power.

The closure of tram routes went on remorselessly. In 1934, Routes 7, 10, and the cutback 14 ceased regular service, although they continued to provide Dockyard Specials for another four years. Only Routes 2, 3, 6 and 12 were now in regular service and this remained the status quo throughout 1935, a year in which 37 double-decker buses were delivered. Route 12 (Prince Rock to Fore Street) was turned over to bus operation on 23 February 1936, and cars stored at Prince Rock depot were then scrapped. The depot was sold in May 1937 — the last subsidiary shed to go — and was later demolished. The site has long been built over and no sign remains today. Route 6 was withdrawn on 4 April 1937, and Route 2 on 9 May. This left only the former Route 9, long redesignated 'P' as a regular, timetabled service, its cars running between Theatre and Peverell Park Corner. It was now known as Route 11 for some incredible administrative reason, but the few cars remaining carried no route number, and in fact had their roller-blind frames removed.

In 1938 the Bath & West Show was held in Central Park, and for the period 25 - 28 May the Peverell trams ran through to Fore Street, track and wires having been retained for workmen's cars. Dockyard Specials continued to run *via* North Road Station and Alma Road until the need of the Great Western Railway to renew Pennycomequick main line bridge (which supported the overhead wires) hastened their end, which came on 25 March 1939. Some workmen's cars were running till the summer between Mutley and North Keyham, but by the outbreak of World War II on 3 September, only the Peverell service was operating, and only twenty-four tramcars remained in stock. The use of trams for peak hour workmen's services over routes normally worked only by buses was an example of Clement Jackson's careful financial policy to clear the Tramway Debt. It obviated the premature purchase of extra buses, many of which would have been idle except at rush hours. In the year ended 31 March 1940, Plymouth Corporation Transport carried 64,321,771 passengers and its traffic revenue was £432,849. Working expenses totalled £317,897 and after providing £80,000 for capital charges and income tax, the surplus was £38,055.

Car No.142 passing the aviary entrance to Beaumont Park, after crossing Friary Bridge, c. 1934. Late survivor of the 'squarefaces', she succombed to the cutter's torch in 1942. Only Stokes' bogies and Exeter and Torquay transfers then remained in service. (Photo — B.Y.Williams)

11

SWANSONG: 1939 - 45

Plymouth, as the largest arsenal in the west of Britain, and possessing the largest naval dockyard in the world, could expect trouble as a prime target if the resistance of France collapsed. When that happened, the war dealt more harshly with the city than anyone had dreamed. The national imperative to make do with existing transport vehicles and to conserve fuel dictated that the only remaining tram route had to continue.

At the outbreak of war twenty-seven cars were still in stock available to work the route: by the end of the war only four were serviceable. The twenty-seven passenger cars were:

'Brown Bears' 151 - 166;
'Square Faces' 142 - 144;
'Ex-Exeters' 2 & 6;
'Ex-Torquays' 10 - 15.

There were also two works cars remaining at Milehouse:

No. 79 (ex-Devonport Brill): Breakdown/towing car;
No. 42 (ex-West Hoe demi): Welding car.

In the first of the 'saturation' air raids on 20 March 1941, tram no. 159 was too severely damaged by blast to be repaired. The same night bogie car 163 was obliterated in the holocaust that destroyed the Central Post Office, Municipal Offices, County Court offices and much of Bedford Street. Evacuated by passengers and crew in Basket Street, 163 was in the centre of this devastated area. Phillip Liddicoat passed through the ruins the following morning and saw that little more than

No. 166 the last of the class, last tram built at Milehouse, and highest-numbered car. By 1945 she was unserviceable and was broken up the following year.

the bogies of 163 remained.

In a later raid at Sherwell, car No. 158 was put out of commission and then entwined with the fallen wires of the wrecked overhead network. She was towed slowly back to Milehouse by No. 79 and repaired. On 30 April the Milehouse depot was severely bombed, with damage centred on the 1931 PCT shed; a number of the cars in stock were rendered unusable. A relic of former days disappeared when on 7 May the former Millbay steam and horse tram depot, which had become Tuckett's sweet factory, was destroyed.

After the raids of March 20 and 21 it was no longer possible to use the tram tracks between St. Andrew's Cross and Theatre, so for the remainder of the war trams for Peverell had to start from an improvised terminus in Old Town Street. Despite these setbacks, the Corporation actually replaced fallen overhead wiring on one or two disused lines where the track was still sound, but no other tram services were operated.

By the summer of 1945 the only serviceable trams were four of Stokes' 'Brown Bears', Numbers 154, 157, 158 and 165. The war ended with VJ day on 2 September, and the decision was taken to terminate the tram service on the 29th, a Saturday. Car No. 158 was chosen to make the final run, leaving Old Town Street at 5.30 p.m. for Milehouse, half-an-hour after the penultimate tram, which was No. 165.

With strip bunting festooned around the upper deck, and large Union Jacks draping her waist and dashes, 158 left Old Town Street with 135 passengers, mostly there by invitation but who all paid fares. Among those on board were: eighty-four-year-old George Slater, who had driven the first Corporation horse tram in 1873; seventy-three-year-old W.A.Smith, who had driven Plymouth's first electric tram in 1889; G.E.Hammett, a passenger on the first electric tram run; Traffic Superintendent Lintern, Assistant Superintendent Knight, and a number of retired former tram crewmen. Two conductors were on duty - R. Bassett and R. Gluvas, and the driver was Herbert Herring, the Corporation's senior motorman. District Inspector Jack Kingdom despatched the car from the desolation of blitzed Old Town Street.

With its considerable load, the war-weary car made rather laboured progress on the two principal gradients of the journey — Tavistock Road and Peverell Park Road. As it passed Hope Baptist Church, a young naval officer, who had been standing casually at the roadside, rushed out and jumped on the crowded rear platform. Conductor

No.158, the car that made Plymouth's last tram journey, seen in war-devastated Old Town Street in 1944. Shown pulling away, north-bound, from the makeshift terminus which was used after severe damage to the track between St. Andrew's and Theatre.

Bassett was a bit taken aback, but the Navy was dear to the public at that time and he wasn't going to be a killjoy. Offered the fare he demurred, but the officer insisted saying,

'Oh, but I must. This will be the last ticket and I shall want the driver to autograph it.'

'Ah, yes,' he replied, 'and you'll find the driver of the first tram on the top deck.'

Having turned Peverell Park Corner, the tram gathered speed down Outlands Road and was soon at Milehouse. Here, ticket no. 7019 (Series L1504), already signed by W.A.Smith, received Herbert Herring's signature, and today is in the care of Plymouth Museum. The anonymous sailor melted into the crowd as the tram was received at the depot by the Lord Mayor and the assembled Transport Committee. A celebration tea followed in the Transport Offices, when it was announced that over the years Plymouth trams had covered over seventy million miles and had carried over 800 million passengers.

No. 158's last run marked the end of an era in Plymouth, but at least the veteran had done it in style. By contrast, when London's last tram, no. 195 of Route 40, reached its destination at New Cross Gate on 5 July 1952, it broke down and suffered the indignity of being towed into the depot by the penultimate car.

Breaking up of the remaining nine passenger cars began before the end of the year, but the Welding Car, No. 42, survived, in a near-derelict state, till the autumn of 1946. The bodies of 151, 155 and 158 were taken to Home Park for pavilions, No. 158 being made a temporary Directors' Stand. Within about four years tram track throughout the city was lifted or buried under resurfacing, except around Derry's Clock, which survived a number of years longer. After dismantling of the overhead wiring, the traction standards in 1948 passed into the ownership of the South Western Electricity Board, and were used as lamp standards.

Little remains today to gladden the eye of the industrial archaeologist, though in the original Devonport company's yard at Milehouse the trackwork is still in place, and the brick sheds still stand. As previously noted, the two Stonehouse company depots can still be seen to the north of Union Street. The redbrick building of the PCT generating substation in Armada Street also remains. At North Hill, on the northgoing pavement of Tavistock Road is a preserved 1898 tram standard worthy of notice. It has cast-iron ribbing and a well-detailed shield with the Plymouth crest and motto, date 1898, and the intertwined initials

PCEW of the Plymouth Corporation Electricity Works. Until the 'seventies there was said to be the body of one tram in a garden at Saltash, and the lower deck of ex-Torquay No. 10 in a field at Yelverton. We have been unable to confirm these locations, and it is reasonable to assume that more than forty years after the trams ceased to run, no recognisable remains of any car still exist.

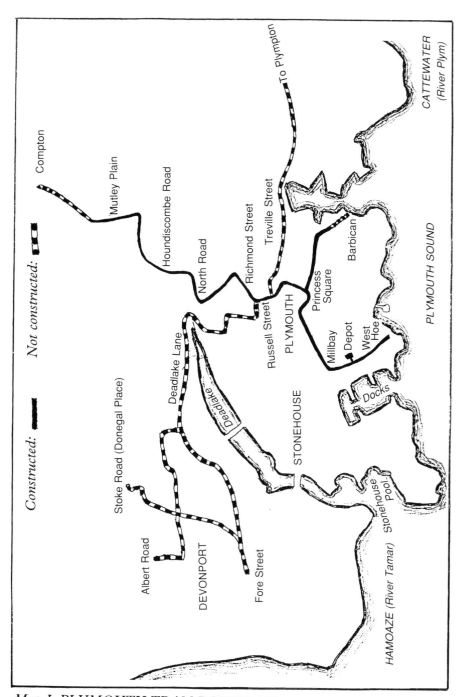

Map I: PLYMOUTH TRAM ROUTE AUTHORISED BY 1882 ACT
— This map shows clearly the grounds for Devonport Corporation's dissatisfaction leading to the Injunction of 1885.

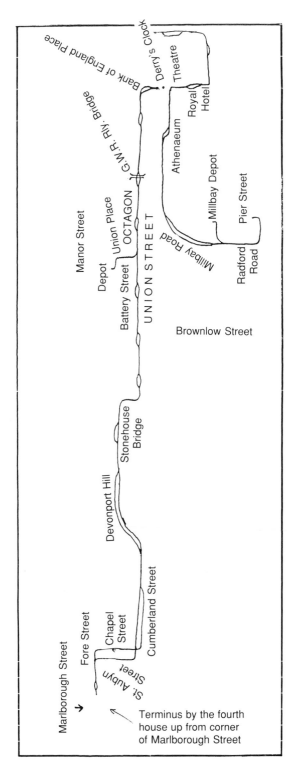

Map II: STONEHOUSE COMPANY'S ROUTE IN 1895 — Of special in this plan are: the crossover in Cumberland Street, and the Pier Street terminus of the West Hoe line.

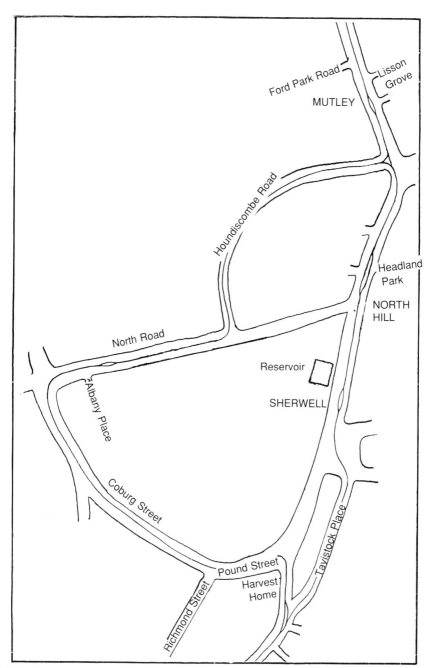

Map III: PLYMOUTH CORPORATION HORSE TRAM ROUTE,
1895: After the laying of the direct (Tavistock Road) line to Compton in
1893, the old Houndiscombe Road track, probably disused, remained for
some years, and the Coburg Street section was re-used for the Pennycomequick
line in 1905.

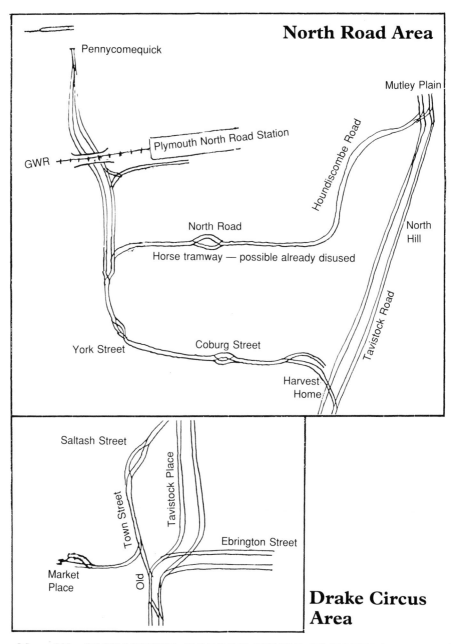

North Road Area

Pennycomequick

Mutley Plain

Plymouth North Road Station

Houndiscombe Road

GWR

North Road

North Hill

Horse tramway — possible already disused

Tavistock Road

York Street

Coburg Street

Harvest Home

Saltash Street

Tavistock Place

Town Street

Ebrington Street

Old

Market Place

Drake Circus Area

Map IV: PLYMOUTH CORPORATION ELECTRIC TRAM ROUTES, 1907 — After the redevelopment of the Tavistock Road — Old Town Street junction as Drake Circus, 1903-4, and the consequent realignment of track, the old line to Market Place, probably disused, remained in situ for some years.

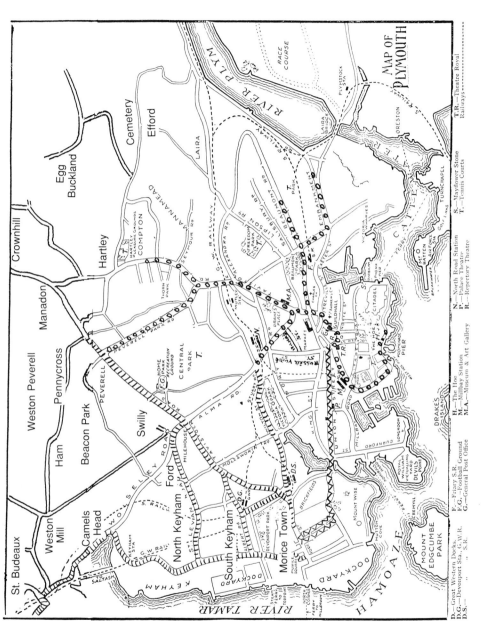

Map V: THE THREE ELECTRIC SYSTEMS, 1901-14 — At the union
of the Three Towns the Devonport Company, though last on the scene, was
working the greatest mileage — eight miles with thirty-three cars, compared
with Plymouth Corporation — six and a half miles with forty-two cars — and
the Stonehouse Company — two and a half miles with fifteen cars.

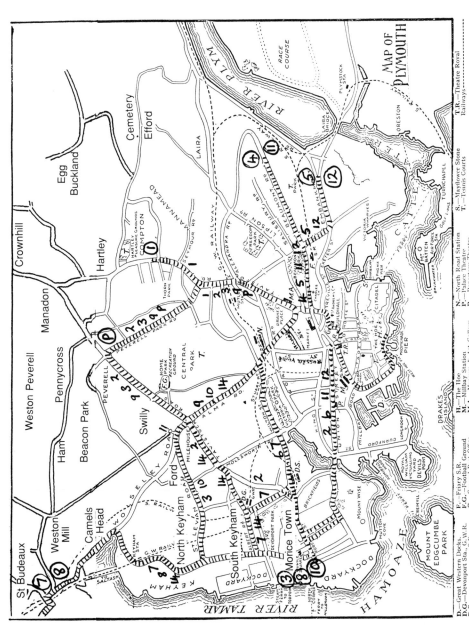

*Map VI: P.C.T. TRAMWAY ROUTE 1922-30 — Not shown are the
North Road Station and Tor Lane spurs, which were lifted during this
period, and the tracks to the five remaining depots.*

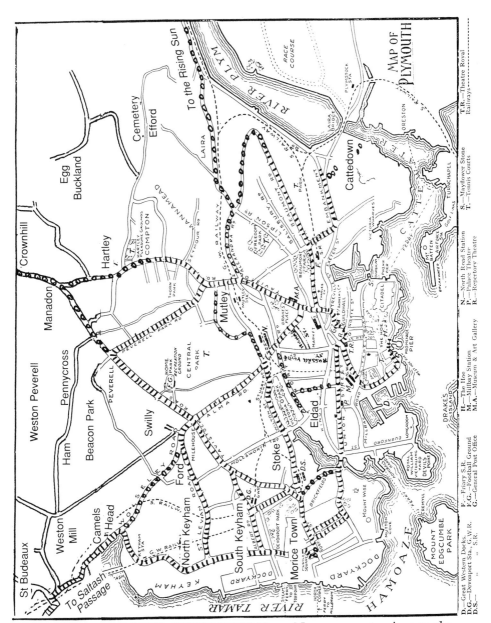

Map VII: PROPOSED EXTENSIONS — Numerous extensions to the
track layout were energetically discussed, both by the Devonport Company
before amalgamation and by Plymouth Corporation thereafter, which never
came to fruition, though some were agreed. Among the least expensive yet
most worthwhile, would have been the Fore Street — Morice Square link-up,
one of several proposals in the early 'twenties. Hartley-Crownhill was
mentioned in an Act; Mutley to Lipson Bridge was agreed but never
implemented. Some of the would-have-been later became bus routes.

111

INTERCHANGE POINTS AND JUNCTIONS

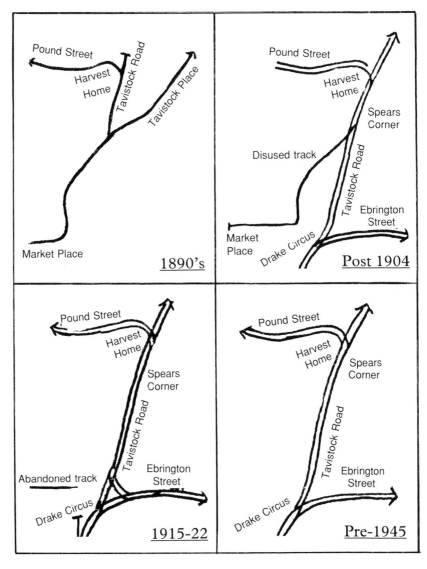

HARVEST HOME — DRAKE CIRCUS

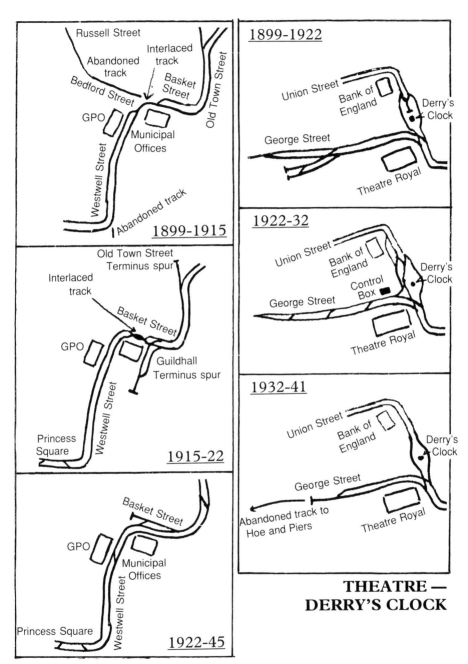

OLD TOWN STREET — PRINCESS SQUARE

THEATRE — DERRY'S CLOCK

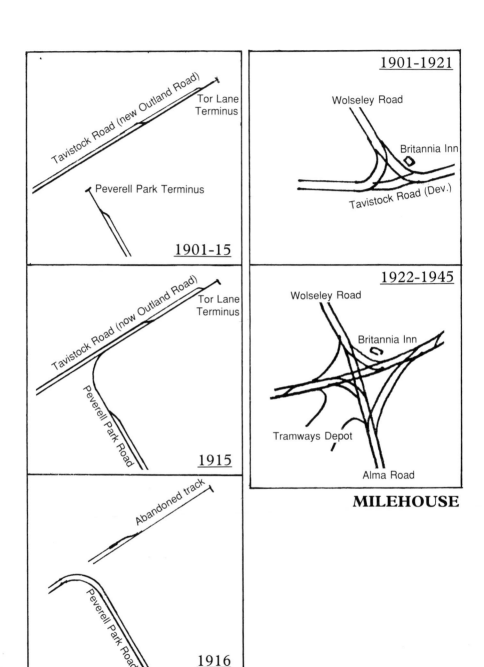

1901-1921

Tor Lane Terminus

Tavistock Road (new Outland Road)

Peverell Park Terminus

Wolseley Road

Britannia Inn

Tavistock Road (Dev.)

1901-15

Tor Lane Terminus

Tavistock Road (now Outland Road)

Peverell Park Road

1915

Abandoned track

Peverell Park Road

1916

1922-1945

Wolseley Road

Britannia Inn

Tramways Depot

Alma Road

MILEHOUSE

TOR LANE — PEVERELL PARK

PENNYCOMEQUICK — NORTH ROAD STATION

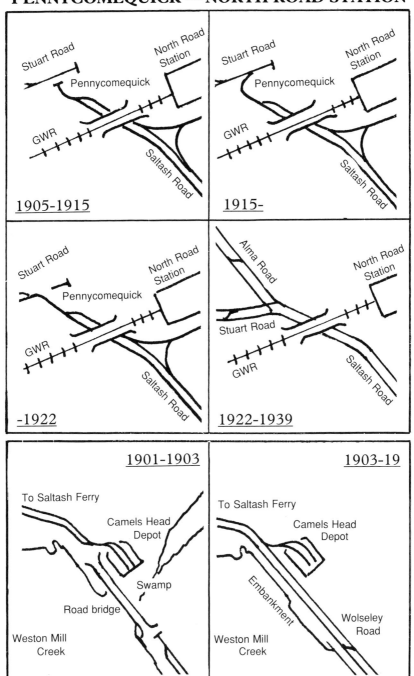

1905-1915

1915-

-1922

1922-1939

1901-1903

1903-19

CAMELS HEAD

FORE STREET

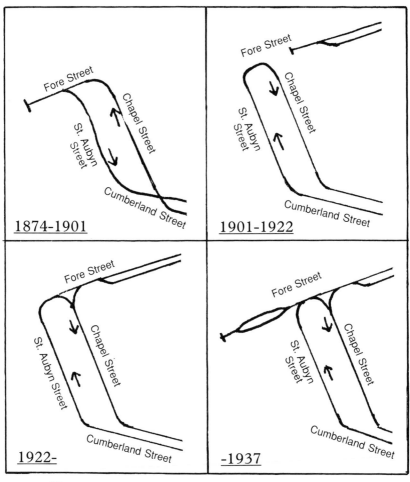

1874-1901

1901-1922

1922-

-1937

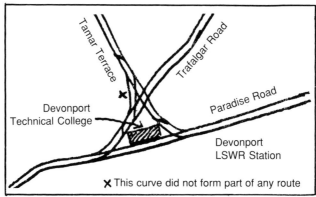

Tamar Terrace

Trafalgar Road

Paradise Road

Devonport
Technical College

Devonport
LSWR Station

✗ This curve did not form part of any route

TAMAR TERRACE

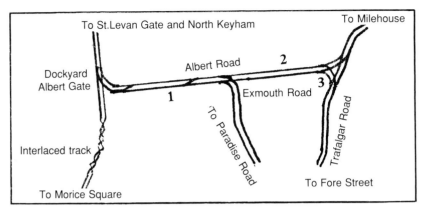

ALBERT ROAD

1 In lower Albert Road tracks were spaced apart, with central poles.
2 Only used by cars to and from depot until Route 14 was opened to use it.
3 Points of this curve were latterly disconnected.

ST. LEVAN ROAD WEST

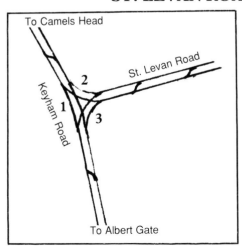

No wires were provided for the connection marked **2**, so the conductor had to leave the trolley on the wire of the line the tram had left until the last moment and then quickly transfer it to the new track. R.N. Barracks special cars used this Route during Navy Weeks.

PLYMOUTH TRAMWAY DEPOTS

1. **Manor Lane, Stonehouse** (Stonehouse Company);
   Tram Sheds and stables; no record of capacity; 1872-1901;
   Now a car repair works.
2. **Market Street, Stonehouse** (Stonehouse Company);
   Workshop, six covered roads and traverser; eighteen cars; 1901-1923;
   Now a tyre warehouse; tracks, etc., in situ.
3. **West Hoe Road, Millbay** (Plymouth Company);
   Four covered roads and a turntable; ten cars; 1893-1907;
   Became Tuckett's sweet factory; blitzed 1941; flats now occupy site.
4. **Belgrave Mews, Mutley** (Plymouth Company);
   Stables for trace horses; no trackwork; 1893-1903;
   Cinema built on the site; now a snooker hall.
5. **Lower Compton Road, Compton** (Plymouth Company);
   Overhaul works and depot; four roads, five in yard; sixteen cars; 1893-1934;
   Now demolished and site redeveloped with flats.
6. **Milehouse Road, Milehouse** (Devonport Company);
   Seven covered roads; thirty-five cars; 1927-1945;
   Sheds still stand, as bus garage; tracks in situ.
7. **Harford Place, Camels Head** (Devonport Company);
   Corrugated iron; two covered roads; two cars; 1901-1930;
   Now demolished and site redeveloped.
8. **Elliott Road, Prince Rock** (Plymouth Corporation);
   Four covered roads; twenty-eight cars; 1899-1936;
   Demolished and built over.

EARLY TRAMWAYS ROLLING STOCK

STONEHOUSE COMPANY — Plymouth, Stonehouse & Devonport Tramways Co., Ltd.

Year Built	Fleet Nos.	Tram Bodies	Trucks	Traction	Disposal
1872	1-8	Builders unknown knifeboard top seating	—	Horses	c.1888
?	1-12	Builders unknown Traverse top seats on later cars	—	Horses	1901
1901	1-15 (no 13)	Dick Kerr; balconied reversed stairs	Brill 21 E	Dick Kerr Electric motors	1922; tram passed to PCT
1916	16	Dick Kerr; balconied direct stairs	Brill 21 E	"	"

PLYMOUTH COMPANIES — Plymouth, Devonport & District Tramways Co., Ltd.

1884	1-5	Open top trailers builders unknown	—	5 Wilkinson 0-4-0 vertical boiler steam engines	1885-89 prob. converted to horse traction
?	1-8	"	—		

Plymouth Tramways Co., Ltd.

1885	1-12	Builders not recorded	—	Horses	Transferred to PCT 1892

Plymouth Corporation Tramways Department

1892	1-12	The above vehicles transferred from PTC	—	Horses	1907
1894	13-17	Milnes; 2 single deckers, 3 open toppers	—	Horses	1907
1895	18-19	Milnes; 2 open toppers	—	Horses	1907
1897	20-25	Bristol; 2 single deck Milnes; 4 open top	—	Horses	1907
1898	26-29	Bristol; 2 single deck Midland; 2 open top	—	Horses	1907

DEVONPORT COMPANY — Devonport & District Tramways Co., Ltd.

1901	1-20	Brill USA; short canopy, direct stairs	Brill	BTH Electric Motors	Transferred to PCT 1914
1901	21-25	Brush; short canopy direct stairs	Brush	"	"
1911	26-29	Brush; full canopy, direct stairs	Brush A	"	"
1911	30-33	Birmingham; balconied, reversed stairs	?	"	"

119

PLYMOUTH CORPORATION TRAMCARS

Nos. 1-6 — 1899	Milne bodies; Peckham Cantilever trucks; Westinghouse motors; short canopy; direct stairs; 4 side-windows; wheel brakes & track brakes. All took part in Opening Day Procession; all fitted for trailer towing; No. 1 exhibited at Tram Conference 1928; Nos. 2, 5, 6, rebuilt with balconies. No. 1 withdrawn 1929; Nos. 2-6, 1924.
Nos. 7-20 1901	Brush bodies; Peckham Cantilever trucks; Westinghouse motors; balconied; reversed stairs; 4 side windows; wheel brakes, track brakes, electric brakes (reverse thrust) on wheels. No. 12 re-trucked to Brill E; No. 16 rebuilt with direct stairs. Nos. 7-11, 13-14, 17-19 withdrawn 1924; Nos. 12, 15, 16, 20 in 1934.
Nos. 21-26 1903	Milne bodies; Peckham Cantilever trucks; Westinghouse motors; balconied; direct stairs; 4 side windows; brakes as Nos. 7-20. No. 22 exhibited at 'All Electric Home' Exhibition. Nos. 21,23,25 withdrawn 1924; Nos. 22, 26 in 1934.
Nos. 27-30 1903	As Nos. 21-26. Nos. 29,30 withdrawn 1924; Nos. 27, 28 in 1934.
Nos. 31-36 1905	Brush bodies; Brill 21E trucks; Westinghouse motors; balconied; direct stairs; 3 side windows; brakes as Nos. 7-20. Seats 24/30; Standard Brush cars. No.34 withdrawn 1924; remainder in 1934.
Nos. 37-42 1906	Brush bodies; Brill 21E trucks; motors as Nos. 31-36; canopied; single deck; 3 side windows; brakes as Nos. 7-20. Seats 22; No. 42 converted to welding car and painted dark green in 1924; Nos. 37- 41 withdrawn 1924, No.42 1945.
Nos. 43-54 1915	Brush bodies; Peckham P22 trucks; Westinghouse motors; balconied; direct stairs; 3 side windows; brakes as Nos. 7-20. Seats 24/30; standard Brush cars; No. 45 later given upholstered seats inside only. All withdrawn 1936.
— 1915	P.C.T. (Compton); single-deck RAILGRINDER; canvas sides. Withdrawn 1935.
Nos. 55-58 1916	Brush bodies; Peckham P22 trucks; Westinghouse motors; balconied; direct stairs; 3 side windows; brakes as Nos. 7-20. Seats 24/30; standard Brush cars. All withdrawn 1935.
Nos. 60-61 1917	Brush bodies; Peckham P22 trucks; balconied; direct stairs; 3 side windows; brakes as Nos. 7-20. Seats 24/30; standard Brush cars.
Nos. 63-65 1901 a 1914	Brush bodies; BTH motors (64=Westinghouse controls); short canopy, direct stairs; 5 side windows; brakes as Nos. 7-20. Seats 22/26; ex-Devonport Company. All withdrawn 1930.
Nos. 66-69 1901 a 1914	Brush bodies; BTH motors; balconied; direct stairs; 4 side windows; brakes as Nos. 7-20. Seats 24/30; ex-Devonport Company Nos. 26-29. All withdrawn 1934.
Nos. 70-73 1911 a 1914	Birmingham bodies; BTH motors; balconied; reversed stairs; 4 side windows; brakes as Nos. 7-20. Ex-Devonport Company Nos. 30-33; Nos. 71, 72 renumbered 41, 42; Nos. 71-73 altered to direct stairs, 1925. No. 70 withdrawn 1925, remainder 1935.

Nos. 74-88	Brill bodies; Brill trucks; BTH motors; short canopy; direct stairs;
1901	brakes as Nos. 7-20.
a 1914	Ex-Devonport Company Nos. 1-20; 74, 79, 83 rebuilt with balconies; 75, 76, 79 converted to single-deck towing/breakdown cars.
	Nos. 77, 78, 80-82, 84-87 withdrawn 1930; Nos. 74, 76, 88 withdrawn 1934.
Nos. 90&92	Brush bodies; Peckham P22 trucks; Dick Kerr motors; balconied; direct stairs; 3 side windows.
	Withdrawn 1936.
Nos. 91&93	PCT body (91), Brush body (93); Dick Kerr motors; balconied; direct stairs;
1920-2	3 side windows (91), 5 side windows (93).
	Ex-Devonport company Nos. 22 & 24.
	Both withdrawn 1935.
Nos. 94-105	Brush bodies; Peckham P22 trucks; Dick Kerr motors; direct stairs; 3 side
1919-20	windows.
	Seats 24/30; standard Brush cars.
	All withdrawn 1936.
No. 112	PCT body; Westinghouse motors; balconied; direct stairs; 3 side windows.
1922	PCT copy of standard Brush car.
	Withdrawn 1935.
Nos. 113-127	Dick Kerr bodies; Brill 21E trucks; Dick Kerr, BTH motors; balconied;
1901	direct stairs; 3 side windows. Ex-Stonehouse cars Nos. 1-16; all except
a 1922	No. 16 converted from reversed to direct stairs; Nos. 114-123 converted to single-enders; No. 119 reverted to double-end, 1931.
	Nos. 114, 115, 117, 118, 120-127 withdrawn 1933, Nos. 113, 116, 119 withdrawn 1935.
Nos. 131-150	EEC bodies; Brill 21E 7'6" trucks; EEC motors; vestibuled; direct stairs; 3 side
1924	windows.
	Seats 24/36; many later given traverse leather seats, inside only.
	Nos. 131-141, 145-150 withdrawn 1938, Nos. 142-144 withdrawn 1942.
No. 151	PCT body; PCT bogies; EEC motors; vestibuled with doors; direct stairs; 4 side
1925	windows; magnetic track hand-operated wheel brakes.
	Altered to single truck.
	Withdrawn 1945.
Nos. 152-166	PCT bodies; PCT bogies; EEC motors; vestibuled; direct stairs; 4 side windows;
1927-8	brakes as No. 151.
	All altered to single truck except Nos. 156, 163, 164.
	No. 163 withdrawn 1941; Nos. 153, 156, 164 in 1942; all others in 1945.
Nos.1-7	Brush bodies; Brill 21E trucks; Westinghouse motors; vestibuled; direct
2nd. series	stairs; 3 side windows; magnetic track hand wheel brake; ex-Exeter 28, 30, 31, 34.
1925-6 a 1931	Nos. 1, 2, 4, 5, 7 withdrawn 1937; Nos. 2, 6 withdrawn 1942.
Nos. 8, 9	Brush bodies; Peckham P22 trucks; Dick Kerr motors; direct stairs; 3 side
1920	windows; brakes as Nos. 1-7.
a 1931	Seats 24/30; ex-Exeter 26, 27; standard Brush cars; originally built as open enders for Plymouth; vestibuled later.
	Both withdrawn 1937.
Nos. 10-15	Brush bodies; Hoffman bogies and roller bearings; Westinghouse motors;
1925	vestibuled; direct stairs; 5 side windows; hand wheel brake, slipper brake.
a 1933	Ex-Torquay Nos 37-42; lower deck seats upholstered.
	All withdrawn 1942.
Nos. 16-21	Brush bodies; Nos. 16, 17 — short wheel-base; BTH motors; balconied;
1906	direct stairs; 3 side windows.
a 1933	Seats 24/30 ex-Torquay, Nos. 7, 9, 10, 16-18 standard Brush cars.
	All withdrawn 1936.

Conductor on Plymouth Corporation Tramcars, pre-1918.

APPENDIX 1:
TRAM CREWS

It is only in the last sixty to seventy years that drivers of any public vehicles have had protection from the weather. Older readers will recall coal delivery carters on open drays with perhaps an old sack around the neck in the rain. So from the beginning of horse trams the driver was out in the open, wearing oilskins. The short canopies over the end platforms of the first electric cars gave the driver virtually no protection at all. Then came full canopies offering a measure of shelter except on the stairway side. Balconies (upper deck and seating extending over full length of car) were a great improvement. Vestibuled platforms only appeared in Plymouth in the mid-1920's.

Drivers worked long unbroken shifts and it was a common sight to see a wife, or more likely a child, waiting at a tram stop at a given time with a can of hot tea and a pudding basin tied up with a red handkerchief for the driver's meal, which he could keep warmed on top of the resistance box. There were no mess rooms for breaks, with hot meals served, in those days.

Remuneration was hardly excessive. In 1914 a conductor was paid 21 shillings for a fifty-four hour week and, in 1919, 55 shillings a week.

It was thought nothing for tram crews to take out a car in the early morning and get off ten hours later without an official break. After duty, whether finishing early or late, the men had to walk home from the depot, and for some men this meant a five mile trudge after a tiring day's work.

APPENDIX 2:
BRAKES ON PLYMOUTH TRAMS

There is little doubt that the braking systems on many of the trams would not pass any test today.

For most of the time Plymouth cars, including those from the Stonehouse and Devonport companies, relied on:

1   Hand-operated brake shoes on the wheels;
2   Electric emergency brake, passing current through the resistances;
3   Hand-worked track brake, forcing hardwood blocks onto the rails.

Many other systems, including London, used a metal track brake with magnetic control, so that when the controller was put into the braking position the resultant current was fed to the magnets, thus attracting the brake shoes to the rail. This was a very powerful brake but it faded off as the speed fell, so that the final stop and hold relied on the wheel brake. It was essential not to apply the wheel brake too hard, especially on a falling gradient; as this could lock the wheels, causing the car to *slide* downhill and, of course, with loss of the magnetic brake. With the advent of big cars with air brakes there often was an automatic valve which eased the pressure of the air brake as soon as the magnetic brake was applied.

The first magnetic track brakes in Plymouth were on the 151 - 166 class (Stokes' 'Brown Bears') but when the Exeter cars were purchased they came so fitted and were used successfully in Plymouth. At one period Route 14 was worked regularly by the Stokes' bogie cars and the descent of Saltash Road past North Road Station was accomplished very smoothly under the magnetic control.

There was also a short period, from 1905, when a few Devonport Brills, and Plymouth car No. 7, were fitted with an extra brake for use on Saltash Road hill but no details of its operation are now available.

The various types of brake employed on Plymouth trams and their modes of operation were as follows:

ELECTRIC BRAKES:

1   Regenerative brakes;
2   Power brakes (working on the motors);
3   Magnetic brakes (working on the rails).

The main characteristic of (1) was that, as the rotation of the wheels created the electric power used for braking, the slower the speed of the car the less efficient the brake became, and the car was brought to a halt by the hand-operated rim brake. Philip Liddicoat recalls:

The drivers of the older cars seemed only to use the electric brake in emergencies, — presumably the result of official instructions. The most spectacular stop I remember was on a Westinghouse open-fronted car — I believe no. 64 — on Mutley Plain. We had just come down from North Hill when a dog ran out from the pavement in front of Mutley Baptist Church. The driver applied full power on the electric brake and we stopped with astonishing suddenness.

Clearly that car had power brakes. But drivers regularly used the regenerative brakes on the Torquay eight-wheelers, which were BTH. Brake action on these cars was inadequate, the mechanical rim-braking system being so low-geared that the driver had to wind the handle round innumerable times to obtain sufficient braking.

The Stokes' bogies and Exeters 1 - 7 had electromagnetic brakes and in their later years these brakes were usually employed as the main braking system: but earlier the 'Brown Bears' were controlled mainly by their Westinghouse Brakes which were very effective.

There seemed to be a relaxation of rules governing the use of brakes in the later 1930's, as until then, for instance, the 131 series rarely used their electric brakes but in the latter years drivers did use them and they appeared very powerful and somewhat harsh. Also in the late 1930's bus drivers were often used on trams and tended not only to drive the cars faster, but to make greater use of the electric brakes. A similar pattern obtained in the use of track-brakes. Where formerly every driver screwed down his track brake before descending the steeper hills, in the latter days the hills were taken sometimes with surprising nonchalance — again particularly by bus drivers. Philip Liddicoat recalls another occasion which was not to be forgotten — this time due not to brake application but to lack of it:

THE TRAMS OF PLYMOUTH

The most hair-raising ride I ever remember was on an open-fronted EEC car coming down the hill from Stoke village to Milehouse. Once past the bend at the top of the hill the driver just cast loose and we shot down at an alarming rate, particularly when we hit the gentle curve at the bottom.

The Torquay eight-wheelers, as previously noted, were underpowered for Plymouth hills. Some drivers would let them race down Peverell Park Road, in order to take the approaching adverse gradient with the greatest possible momentum. Even so these cars would drop to not much more than walking-pace by the top of the hill above St. Gabriel's Church.

NON-ELECTRIC BRAKES:

1   Handwheel-operated track brakes;
2   Brass-handle worked brake applying brake shoes to wheels.

The 'sledge' or 'slipper' track brakes — wooden blocks attached to a steel assembly — were used only for checking the speed of a car descending a hill. The handwheel was usually combined with the other mechanical brake control, the track-brake wheel column being hollow and the rim-brake control column being housed within it. On some cars however (*e.g.* the 21 series) the two columns were separate.

The main non-electric brake which on all trams except the Stokes' bogies and Exeter BTH cars, was the principal stopping and retarding system, was operated by a rotating brass handle whose column, as stated, was within the column of the track-brake control wheel which was of black steel.

There was a large foot-operated ratchet at the base of the column, to hold the rim brake on. The motorman had a cloth in his right hand with which he held the brake lever. The trackbrake wheel was always operated by both hands.

The Exeter BTH cars had no sledge track-brakes and their free-standing rim-brake handles appeared of heavier construction. The Stokes' bogie-cars, being fitted with Westinghouse air brakes, had an auxiliary mechanical braking system operating on the same rim-brake shoes. This was worked by a rotating handle, usually detached when not in use, whose axle was horizontal and fitted into a red-painted column near the air brake control.

REFERENCES

Wilson, Frank E. and Marshall, Percival: *The British Tram.*
Klapper, Charles: *The Golden Age of Transport* (David and Charles, 1974).
Belt and Gilham: *Great British Tramway Networks* (L.R.T.League, 1957)
Moseley, Brian: *The History of Transport in Plymouth* (Mosbic, 1964)
Williams, B.Y.: *Lecture Notes* (Unpublished)
Gill, Crispin: *Plymouth: A New History* (David and Charles, 1979)
Trams to Bus (Unpublished Notes, PCT)
The Tramway and Railway World (May 1922 issue)
Tramway Review Magazine (Summer 1980 issue)
Gentry, P.W.: *The Tramways of the West of England* (L.R.T.League, 1960)
Western Daily Mercury; Western Evening Herald; Western Independent; Western Morning News.

ACKNOWLEDGEMENTS

Stan Daymond of Mutley; Ern Evans of Keyham; Frank Graham of Mt. Gold; Jack Kingdom of Plymstock; Philip Liddicoat of Glenholt; B.Y.Williams of London for loan of the originals of all the photographs reproduced in this book and for advice and help freely given during its preparation.
National Tramway Museum, Crich; Plymouth Central Library; Plymouth Citibus Ltd.

More Books from Ex Libris Press:

IRON HORSE TO THE SEA
Railways in South Devon
John Pike

John Pike's story is a fascinating journey through the many years of rail travel in the district. The author is a former chief librarian of Torbay and lectures regularly on his subject: his enthusiasm is infectious. This written account features much new material, including some remarkable and often amusing incidents which throw fresh light upon the social history of the rail era. In addition, the majority of the many illustrations are here published for the first time and certainly add great interest.

159 pages   Fully indexed   Price £3.95

TALL SHIPS IN TORBAY
A brief maritime history of Torquay, Paignton and Brixham
John Pike

In this book are the stirring events of history: the defeat of the Spanish Armada, the capture of Napoleon, the landing of William, Prince of Orange. Here too are less familiar episodes: ruthless pirates and their struggles against the Revenue men, the press gangs which terrorised the male population, the provision of support services for the British Fleet anchored in the Bay, local shipbuilding, emigration to the Colonies, the development of the Coastguard Service and the modern fishing industry and much more. *Tall Ships in Torbay* is expertly researched and well documented; it is also fully illustrated with an outstanding collection of pictures.

142 pages   Fully indexed   £3.95

WEST COUNTRY TREASURY
A Compendium of West Country Lore and Literature, People and Places
Alan Gibson and Anthony Gibson

This remarkable collection spans the Western Counties geographically and chronologically. The authors approach their many and varied subjects in a lively and original manner which reveals their lifetimes' fascination with all aspects of West Country life.
Here are poets and preachers, miners and murderers, sailors and chimney-sweeps, philanthropists and engineers, travellers and writers. Some will be entirely new to you, and you will enjoy the authors' fresh insights into the lives of those which are familiar.

304 pages   Fully indexed   £7.50

The above books may be obtained from your local bookshop or from the publisher, post-free. at 1 The Shambles, Bradford on Avon, Wiltshire, BA15 1JS.
A current list of titles will be sent upon request.